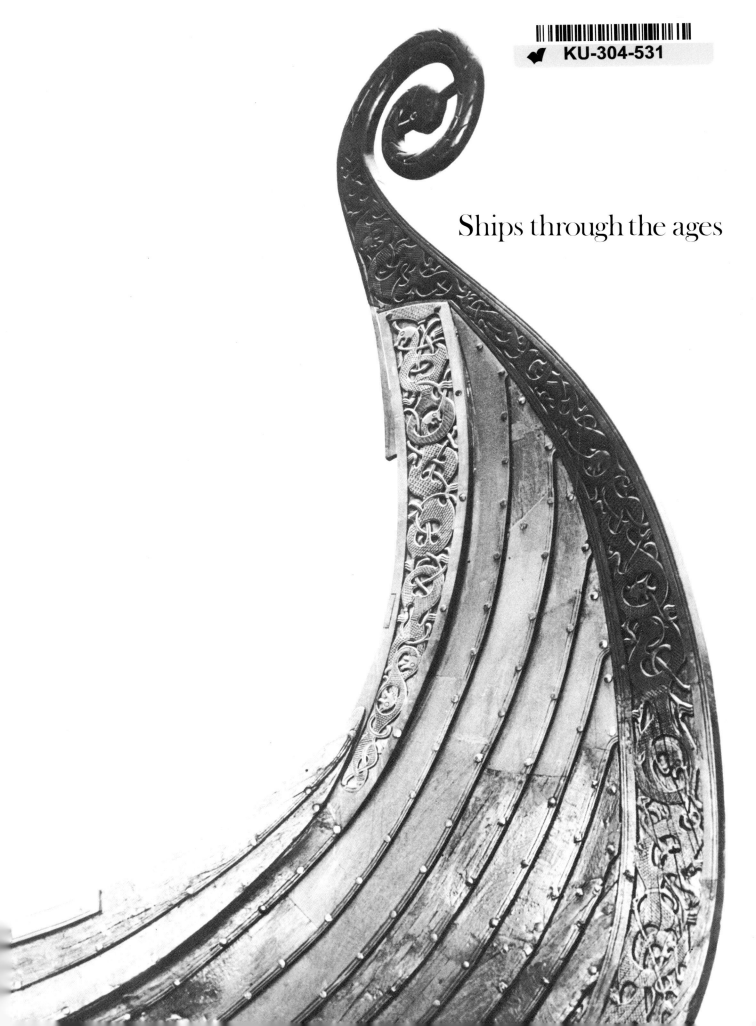

Ships through the ages

Ships through the ages

Douglas Lobley

OCTOPUS

Special artwork by Bill Robertshaw
Designed by Geoff Cloke

This edition published 1975 by
Octopus Books Limited
59 Grosvenor Street, London W1

ISBN 0 7064 0482 3

© 1972 Octopus Books Limited

Produced by Mandarin Publishers Limited
Toppan Building, Westlands Road
Quarry Bay, Hong Kong

Printed in Hong Kong

Contents

Introduction

This book is a compression of 6,000 years of the history of the ship from tree trunk dug-out to nuclear liner – a story which resembles a family tree with innumerable branches, becoming most numerous during the years from the early nineteenth century. This book cannot hope to describe the multiplicity of ship types that were built in step with technological development. The aim has been to describe a cross-section of passenger liners, cruise liners, and cargo carriers.

To many people the story of early ships has a special fascination, especially the ships of the Egyptian Pharoahs, the Viking ships, and the ships of the fifteenth century when the full-rigged sailing ship came into being. But perhaps the most exciting period of all was the era of the clipper ship, between 1845 and 1865, when the sailing ship fought for survival. The issue was never in doubt. Eventually steam was the victor. But the clipper ships left behind them almost inexhaustible records of their voyages.

It is difficult to single out individual trades in a book which covers many incidents and developments in the history of sail and steam. One of my own interests is the North Atlantic trade. British and European shipping companies carried many thousands of new citizens to the United States and Canada during the developing period. Samuel Cunard set the course of the first regular service across the Atlantic Ocean. One has to think also of Brunel, who, with Scott Russell, designed the *Great Eastern* in the late 1850s, a ship which was years ahead of her time.

Indeed, the century which has past since that period has been a revolutionary age for ships of all classes – paddle-wheelers, ironclads, dreadnoughts driven by steam turbines, nuclear submarines, passenger and specialist cargo ships bearing ever more sophisticated equipment. A remarkable story which continues still.

DOUGLAS LOBLEY

First beginnings

Papyrus boats, so much a feature of early Egyptian boat-building, had their counterparts as far away as Lake Titicaca in South America, where balsa was and still is used for the construction of boats.

Egyptian workers shaping a
small river boat from short
planks, *c* 2000 BC.

Throw a stone into a river and it sinks without trace.
Throw a branch of a tree and it floats smoothly down-
stream. In the shadowy period of prehistory two
hundred thousand years ago, primitive man learnt
these things. He saw that when the river was in flood
after a storm whole trees remained afloat. He learnt
that they had enough buoyancy to support his own
weight. He found that a tree shorn of its branches,
instead of drifting aimlessly, could be made to move
faster by paddling with a branch, and be given direction by movements of his feet. It is not too fanciful
to speculate that after a downpour prehistoric man's
animal-skin clothing, hung up to dry on a tree-
branch paddle, could have provided the first primitive sail.

There is no telling who in the world first made
these discoveries, or on what continent. But it is
reasonable to suppose that throughout the earth's
populated land-masses – which, unknown to him,
were far exceeded in area by the oceans and seas –
man, in widely differing climates, began to discover
which of nature's creations would float. Thousands
of years may have separated the use of solid trees as

'boats' and the first hollowed-out tree trunks or dug-
outs, or the bunches of reeds that made the first raft.
What is certain is that today on the upper reaches of
tributaries of the River Amazon, balsa, that lightest
of woods, fashioned into the type of raft to which it
gave its name, continues to carry a still primitive
people and their goods.

Proof of the enduring nature of primitive boats in
backwaters is to be found in Africa. Few will have
heard of Lake Abaya (sometimes marked as Lake
Margherita) 230 miles south of Addis Ababa, capital
of Ethiopia, and still fewer of the island on the lake
called Gidicho, whose inhabitants continue to use
one of the most interesting boats of all time – the
hobolo. So far as is known the hobolo exists nowhere
else. Simply to see one is to wonder how it can float,
for the hobolo is uncaulked and water can find its
way between the curved baulks of ambatch wood
that form the hull. Ambatch is as light as balsa and
the hobolo has enough buoyancy to carry several
people and a cargo, these being kept dry by bundles
of sticks laid in the boat to above water-level. The
hobolo is propelled by a gopashi, a long, curved pole

An Egyptian sea-going boat of c 2600 BC, built for the Mediterranean. Notice the triple steering sweeps, the bank of paddles and the heavy mast.

ending in a block of ambatch wood to which are attached two tusk-like balancers; the gopashi works on the principle that the thrust needed to force the light wooden block under water provides adequate motion.

The passage of time, no matter in how many thousands of years it is measured, can leave undisturbed a whole way of living. In common with that of entire civilizations, progress in the shape and size of ships sometimes leapt forward, only to be followed by a period of stagnation.

It was in Egypt and Mesopotamia, a mere six thousand years ago, that man first began to leave conscious records. In Egypt, papyrus, then growing in abundance on the banks of the Nile, had at least two significant uses. It provided scrolls on which to record events, and material to build the first river craft, layer upon layer of papyrus being bound together to form a sheath-like raft. But not until a further five hundred years had passed, in about 3500 BC, did drawings of boats (as distinct from rafts) begin to appear in the wall paintings of the rapidly developing Egyptian civilization. Still built of papy-

rus, they were roughly U-shaped. Each member of the crew had a paddle – it was to be a thousand years before boats were pictured with oarsmen – and the boats were steered from the stern by a larger paddle. Their sterns swept upwards and their sharp prows, also bent upwards to make landing easier in shallow water, were surmounted by heads of fierce-looking beasts to ward off evil spirits and frighten the enemy. For thousands of years the ornamented prow remained a feature of Mediterranean boats and galleys, eventually to be perpetuated in the elaborate and often beautiful figureheads of sailing ships. Even today the gondolas of Venice reflect the high, ornamented prows of the river boats of five thousand years ago.

Next came masts and a single sail. Initially, the mast was placed well forward in the boat and its single sail gave extra speed as the boat ran before the wind. The Egyptians made good use of the wind which in the region of the Nile blows in a constant direction for months on end – though the return trip was sheer hard work for the crew. The then useless mast and sail were stowed in the bottom of

11

Ships from Queen Hatshepsut's expedition which *c* 1500 BC sailed south down the Red Sea from Egypt to the land of Punt, an ancient territory probably in the region of modern Somalia. This nineteenth-century reconstruction shows two ships being loaded with produce and animals. The massive masts and upturned sterns mark the ships as having been constructed for a long voyage. Steered by two sweeps lashed together, each ship had fifteen oarsmen on either side.

the boat, for the Egyptians had yet to learn the use of rigging for tacking.

Around 3000 BC Egyptian boats, by that time built of wood from a source further up the Nile, had ventured seaward in the eastern Mediterranean. It was a perfect proving ground for early ships – a virtually enclosed sea, dotted with islands and peninsulas separated by comparatively short sea voyages. There was a constant interchange of ideas and customs between the different peoples inhabiting the area and, inevitably, trials of strength took place. Successive pharaohs embarked upon foraging expeditions that today would be called cut-and-run raids. One such expedition was instigated in about 2740 BC by Pharaoh Sahure of the Fifth Dynasty: he raided Phoenician territories along the coastal strips of what

are now Syria, the Lebanon and Israel, returning with booty and prisoners.

The Phoenicians were the first true merchant adventurers. They were not a warlike people, and it is ironic that although in later generations they were to venture outside the Mediterranean to Britain and western Europe, they left no written or pictorial records of their history. Some historians maintain that they were too busy trading and making money to find time for writing and painting. Their achievement was rather to spread, by the audacity of their seafaring, the discoveries of other civilizations.

Their ships were of more advanced design than Egypt's sea-going vessels, which were essentially Nile boats adapted for the open sea. The Egyptians were by nature mainly river sailors, confining their

sea expeditions to short journeys in the eastern Mediterranean. However, some noteworthy ventures did take place under Egyptian leadership. One of these was organized by Queen Hatshepsut, who, as co-regent with Thotmes III, despatched a peaceful expedition to the land of Punt, returning with silks, fabrics and spices. The ships of her expedition and its bounty are commemorated on the walls of the Queen's temple at Deir el-Bahari, opposite Thebes. Hatshepsut was a strong-minded woman who for twenty years dominated her husband; when she died in about 1470 BC, Thotmes began a series of territorial conquests which revealed his genius as a strategist. He subdued the territories of the Near East above Gaza; but to the north the Syrians held out at Kadesh. Thotmes deduced that he needed a naval base close to Kadesh to avoid long forced marches overland from Egypt. Considering the date, this was a brilliant strategic conception. He assembled a great fleet and put his forces ashore at Arvad in northern Phoenicia, achieving a decisive victory. Thotmes had anticipated by over 3,400 years the use of ships for invasion, a strategic principle adopted with such success by Britain and the USA in the Second World War.

After 1200 BC Egyptian interest in ships and the sea diminished, although what is thought to be the first picture of a sea battle was found in the tomb of Rameses III (died c1158 BC): it shows Egyptian ships, manned by skilled Phoenician seamen, driving back an invasion force of tribes expelled from the lands bordering the eastern Mediterranean. The latter were collectively termed the 'Peoples of the Sea' and included the Achaeans, Danaans and Philistines. The battle can be dated at around 1190 BC. Another major source were the treasures of Tutankhamen's tomb: discovered as recently as 1922, the tomb yielded a fleet of models including a remarkably detailed one of the boat in which the young pharaoh sailed the Nile in about 1380 BC. Thereafter Egyptian civilization declined – and with it the zest to keep detailed records of its history.

In the earlier years of the last millennium BC pressures of population compelled the Greeks to colonize and settlements grew in southern Italy, Crete and Cyprus. These activities required ships that could carry passengers and cargo. Drawings or pictures of such merchant ships are scarce but the Greeks appear to have favoured types that relied entirely on sails. Their hulls stood fairly high out of the water and were topped by a primitive superstructure in the shape of a trellis. This enabled more cargo to be loaded and the passengers had the protection of the trellis (later to be more precisely termed a bulwark) to shield them from falling over the side when the ship lurched in a rough sea. Greece imported two-thirds of her corn supply by such methods. She was also short of domestic timber suitable for shipbuilding, and so had her ships built at Tyre, close to the cedars of Lebanon – a practice followed later by the Romans.

In 499 BC came the collision of Greece with Persia. The Persian Wars lasted for fifty years and, in the history of ships, this period marks the first moves to design ships for special functions. For peaceful pursuits there evolved over the next seven centuries the trading or merchant ship, so that by AD 200 the ancestor of the English 'tub' or 'round ship' and of the French *vaisseau rond* had made its appearance. They were imprecisely documented and only after a gap of a thousand years, in the early thirteenth century, did the city seals of seaports begin to record the appearance of trading ships.

The Greek and other Mediterranean trading ships of 500 BC were of course useless for waging war. They were dependent on the whim of the wind, sluggish in movement and incapable of rapid manoeuvre.

The fighting ship for Mediterranean seas was the *galley*: she was long, lean and low; furthermore, being propelled by oars, she had the advantage of manoeuvrability whatever the state of tide or wind. But a galley had to be lightly built, and of shallow draught, and therefore could carry very little cargo. On the other hand the galley, whether she was a *bireme* or a *trireme*, that is, with two or three banks of

A bas-relief found at Ostia of a Roman trading ship of AD 200, little different from the deep-hulled ship that carried St Paul to Ostia. Features include the stocky, slanting mast at the bows on which was bent the artemon sail that helped keep the ship before the wind; and massive side rudders.

Greek war galleys were known as biremes, triremes, quadremes and quinquiremes, indicating two, three, four and five banks of rowers. Here is an impression of how five rows of oarsmen might have been disposed.

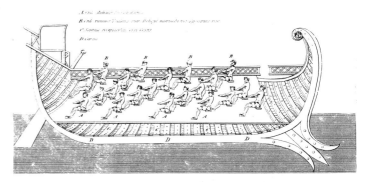

rowers, was a powerful battering ram in herself because of her specially designed beak. Incidentally, this beak, brought up to date, can be seen in the ram bows of steel-built warships of the 1880s, and in the dreadnoughts of the first decade of the twentieth century.

The galley in fact remained the fighting ship of the Mediterranean for some two thousand five hundred years – up to the battle of Lepanto in 1571, when

Building a coracle, a boat of ancient origins still used in Wales for salmon fishing.

1. fashioning withy (or willow) staves for a coracle's framework.

2. the completed framework and single paddle.

Spanish galleys defeated the Turks, the last sea fight between ships propelled mainly by man himself.

One popular misconception should be laid to rest at this stage. Because the Mediterranean is a closed sea, it does not follow that its gales are mild compared with those of the North Atlantic. There is a difference, of course, but the Roman galleys that sailed to the northern lands survived the westerlies even though they took a hammering. The Romans soon discovered that the boat builders of the north used heavier timbers.

Apart from minor refinements added after experience, the trading ship remained unchanged during five centuries of Roman domination. The seaport serving Rome, the hub of the empire, was Ostia, on the River Tiber. Valuable clues to the shape of a Roman trading ship were found at Pompeii, dating from about AD 50; and carvings (c AD 200) at Utica, near Carthage, and in Ostia itself, provided sufficient evidence for the French nautical scholar, Dr Jules Sottas, to construct a model. Her hull is deep

enough to contain capacious holds for cargo. She is shown with two masts, although the small mast in the bows looks more like the bowsprit that it was to become in later centuries. This mast was an important advance, for it carried a foresail called an artemon that helped to keep the ship on a steady course before the wind. It was just this type of foresail, by the way, that steadied the ship taking St Paul to Ostia when she was in danger of foundering.

Following the decline of Greece and the conquest of Carthage, Roman power in Europe on land and sea was to endure for five hundred years. It is furthermore true to say that Rome founded her shipbuilding skill on Carthaginian experience, itself inherited from the Phoenicians. On one important occasion, an accident of war and weather presented the Romans with an almost intact Carthaginian galley, driven ashore on a Roman beach. The Romans improved their shipbuilding knowledge from study of the style of rig, arrangement of the thwarts for the oarsmen, and positions for the legionaries; they found also

3. a finished coracle being carried in traditional style.

4. preparing to net salmon on the River Teifi. The net, with a four-inch mesh, is stretched between the two coracles and used as a trawl.

that the galley had more effective steering, using large sweeps with connecting poles that passed through the hull – the nearest yet to a rudder. From this find on a beach grew a new generation of fighting galleys, culminating in strongly built and richly carved craft surmounted at the stern by a fighting platform or 'castle'.

After his invasion of Gaul and Britain in 55 BC, Julius Caesar decribed the boats he encountered. The hulls were flatter and heavily built to withstand frequent grounding in the shallows of estuaries and beaches on the English Channel, where the rise and fall of tide can be as much as twenty-five feet (whereas the Mediterranean is close to being tideless). Caesar was evidently moved by the skilled and practical construction of these craft and described them at length. It is worth quoting a passage from his commentary on the Gallic Wars: 'The prows were raised very high and in like manner the sterns. The ships were built wholly of oak and designed to endure any force and violence whatever: the benches,

which were made of planks a foot in breadth, were fastened by iron spikes the thickness of a man's thumb; the anchors were secured fast by iron chains instead of cables and for sails they used skins and dressed leather'.

Even as Caesar was extolling the merits of contemporary British sea-going ships, *coracles* were widely used in Wales. After two thousand years they continue to do useful work, in particular on the River Teifi which runs through the town of Cardigan to the sea. The coracle is mainly employed in salmon netting. In the village of Cenarth, coracles are fashioned with great skill; they are simple craft but perfectly adequate for their task.

On the other side of the known world the Arabs were already advanced seafarers; they knew, for instance, how to make best use of the monsoon season of winds to help speed their ships to India. This enterprise alone is enough to cancel out the familiar picture of the Arab as a nomadic figure circumscribed by the desert; and who, when he did put to

1. The hobolo of Lake Abaya in Ethiopia, one of the lightest and most buoyant boats of all time, also one of the oldest.

2. on Lake Chad in Africa papyrus boats are used that are very similar to those on Lake Titicaca in South America.

3. an Arab dhow, her great lateen sail dominating her tiny hull, off the island of Djerba in the Mediterranean.

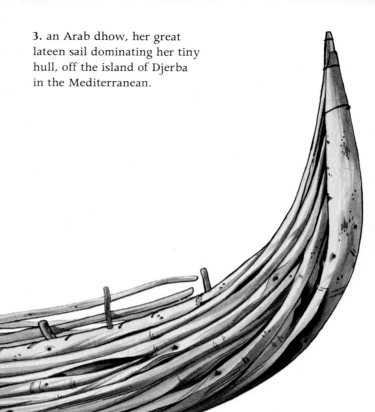

1

2

A Nile trading boat, unchanged in design for centuries. The exceptionally large yard of the lateen rig helps the boat to catch the wind.

sea, had only one kind of ship – the *dhow*. The word 'dhow' has passed into the English language as the name of the Arab sea-going ship, but in reality it includes a number of vessels of differing shapes and usages.

However, tempting though it is to follow up the variety of craft that are to be found on the immensely long coastline of the Arabian peninsula, let alone its estuaries and marshes, to do so would be to lose track of our main purpose – to describe the more important type of craft or ship that directly contributed to the extension of man's knowledge of his world.

How did the Arabs become such sophisticated seamen? There is every reason to believe that the civilization of Mesopotamia of around 3500 BC, in the region between what is now Baghdad and the Persian Gulf, passed on to the Arabs knowledge that helped them to understand that the stars, particularly the Pole star with its constant elevation, could aid them in traversing long stretches of sea *out of sight of land*.

The Arabs developed a device which they named Al-Kemal, meaning a guide-line, to determine what today is called latitude and is found by the use of a sextant. Al-Kemal is described by the Swedish author Per Collinder as no more than a small piece of horn shaped like a parallelogram, with pieces of string attached, knotted at intervals to correspond with observations made by the Arab navigator of the relative positions of the Pole star and the horizon.

Not only were the Arabs advanced in navigation. Another widely supported theory maintains that the Arabs, by trial and error, gradually evolved the lateen sail, a sail with great flexibility of movement, and that it was they who introduced it to Mediterranean seafarers. Basically the lateen sail is a triangle, bent on to a very long curved yard attached to a short mast. It is a 'loose-footed' sail and can be adjusted quickly to a variety of angles to catch the wind; and when a squall comes up with customary Mediterranean swiftness, the lateen can be furled just as rapidly. In a sea area without trade winds, such as the Mediterranean, the lateen sail was a great boon.

20

Lateen-rigged Indian river
boats; these bear a close
resemblance to Nile craft.

Escape from the dark ages

The high, curved prow of the Oseberg ship (c 800), discovered near Oslo in 1903.

The term 'Dark Ages' is a familiar label for the dreary period in European history that followed the collapse of the Roman Empire. In Britain the first gleam of light suggesting a revival of interest in ship design came in the reign of Alfred the Great (AD 871 – 99). But first it is interesting to see what had happened to the shape of ships in the far north in pre-Roman times, and to look at one of the most controversial groups of peoples in the history of the ship – the Vikings.

When one has absorbed a part of the great volume of facts and pictures left by the Egyptian and Mesopotamian civilizations, it is something of a surprise to find that, in the north, actual relics of craft, built long before written records, are the chief clue to early boat building. The Scandinavians did not begin to write on parchment until the middle of the eleventh century. Possibly the best preserved example of the northern dug-out was discovered in 1886 at Brigg in Lincolnshire, England. This craft is now in the museum at Hull.

Northern craft of the first century AD were double-ended: viewed from the broadside, bow and stern were identically shaped. Not only in this feature did they differ from the Mediterranean ships of Carthage: their hulls, too, were stronger; this was because the planks of timber overlapped and were nailed together. This is kown as *clinker built*. In Mediterranean ships the planks met edge to edge to form a smooth surface. These were *carvel built*. A well preserved specimen from the north, built about AD 200, was found in 1863 at Nydam in Denmark and is now in Kiel. Only in dimensions does she resemble a galley, being both long and narrow – seventy-six feet long and eleven feet wide. The Nydam ship was not built for the sea. Not until the eighth century did Scandinavian ships begin to carry sails; their hulls were then lengthened and deepened and bulwarks were added.

A leap in time to AD 800 brings the Vikings to the scene. The Vikings – a collective term for the peoples of many Nordic races – too often have been described chiefly as dominating a three-centuries-long eruption of plunder, rapine and terrorism on the seas, between 800 and 1100. But their contribution to ship design was important and long-lasting. Their ships were based on the example of Nydam, built six hundred years earlier. Later they produced ships stout enough to brave the wild climate and great seas of the North Atlantic ocean, the high latitudes of Iceland and Greenland.

Their funeral customs resembled those of the pharaohs of ancient Egypt. A chieftain was made ready for his voyage to Valhalla by being laid aboard a fully equipped ship which was then buried in the earth. Two ships, remarkably preserved, were unearthed within fourteen miles of each other close to the Oslo Fjord in Norway in 1880 and 1903. Both ships have been fully restored and are in the Hall of the Vikings outside Oslo. The 1880 discovery, at Gokstad, is particularly interesting because her design reveals that she was built for the open sea, as was proved when a replica crossed the Atlantic in 1893 to appear at an exhibition in Chicago. The passage lasted twenty-eight days and during part of the voyage the ship reached a speed of ten knots. Experts date the Gokstad ship at about 900.

The carved and decorated ship found at Oseberg was built about a century earlier and may have been the tomb of Queen Asa of Norway. The hull contained the skeletons of two women and was loaded with domestic paraphernalia, from lamps and looms to kitchen utensils; whereas the Gokstad ship was a chieftain's grave and contained weapons, fragments of three smaller boats and the skeletons of twelve horses and six dogs. These ships were trading ships and not the longships in which the Vikings sailed on conquest. Longships were up to 150 feet in length; unfortunately not enough relics survive for purposes of reconstruction.

Despite a lack of domestic records, Viking emigration to the far west is better documented, thanks to the Sagas. Here the key question is how far west the Vikings went. That they reached Iceland and Greenland is undisputed. But the two Icelandic Sagas which

tell this part of the story go on to describe a country of lush green vegetation, discovered by a Viking mariner with the appropriate name of Leif the Lucky. He called the new land Vinland, or Wineland, the land of the grapes. There is mention in the Vinland Sagas of contact with Indian tribes, indicating that the Vikings did in fact set foot on North American soil five hundred years before the great voyages of Christopher Columbus's day.

It is timely here to return to Alfred the Great. A scholar, law-giver and soldier, he was the first British king to realize that his island country was a fortress in itself, dependent on ships for commerce and defence. He is considered 'the father of the English navy', which can be misunderstood for there were rulers before him who had fighting ships under their command. But Alfred had an innate sense of the strategy and tactics of sea power. For instance, by building fighting ships with a higher freeboard, he gave his men the advantage of looking down on the enemy; he also appreciated that one of the duties of a fleet was to entice an enemy into fighting at sea before he had a chance to set foot ashore.

Portrayals of English and Norman ships in the Bayeux Tapestry show that the specifications of Alfred's ships of 897 had been followed and were still in use at the Norman conquest in 1066. A gap then occurs in our knowledge of the development of ships, until about 1400. Only details on city seals provide

information, and this is imprecise because of their small scale. Yet the seals of Dover, Sandwich, Hythe, Winchelsea, Hastings and Rye are of historic interest.

An important aspect of ship design is the interplay between trading and fighting ship. At one period they are indistinguishable. Then they separate – mark the difference in appearance between Roman trading ships and war galleys. Now again comes a prolonged period of some four hundred years when trading and fighting ships outwardly look alike. This period lasted until technological refinements to the steam engine, the iron hull, and to explosive and incendiary shells, separated completely the two types of ship.

The city seals of the thirteenth and fourteenth centuries show the continuation of double-ended ships with side rudders. What remains uncertain is the date of the first stern rudder, perhaps the most significant technical development of the period. One piece of evidence is a carving on the twelfth-century marble font, from Tournai, Belgium, in the Cathedral at Winchester, Alfred the Great's capital. This shows a ship with what is unmistakably a stern rudder.

An interesting feature of ships of the Middle Ages are the 'castles' built at bow and stern to adapt trading ships for war. There were three castles: the forecastle (soon to be known as the foc'sle), the aftercastle (which became the poop) and the topcastle which remained for a long time as it was, finally to

A selection of city seals from the thirteenth and fourteenth centuries: these provide a rare source of information on ship design of that period.

1. Seal of Hythe: the fore and after castles were then so insignificant that they were lower than the bow and stern posts. The swarm of fish suggests that this boat was a predecessor of the fishing drifter, but there are no nets visible to prove it.

2. Seal of Hastings: two ships appear here, but the picture otherwise features a single ship. There is no forecastle, only an aftercastle. Notice that in all the city seals the ships are clinker built.

3. Seal of Sandwich: this type of ship and her immediate predecessors carried English forces to the Third Crusade. The fore and aftercastles are temporary structures, as also is the topcastle on the mast. The three 'rubbing cleats' on the hull are for protection when mooring the ship alongside a quay. Observe the small lifeboat amidships and the beginnings of a bowsprit.

1   2   3

4. Seal of Winchelsea: the seal shows the crew at work. The ship is weighing anchor: two men in the bows haul on the cable to help two others at the windlass; another member of the crew goes aloft to set sail. The trumpeters sound departure, and the steersman is ready at the side-rudder.

5. Seal of Dover: although the fore and aftercastles have become permanent features, and overlap the bow and stern posts, and there is a topcastle, the ship retains the side-rudder. The engraver has put it on the wrong side, forgetting that a pressing of the seal would be reversed. This will have been among the last of the double-ended ships.

6. Seal of Rye: this ship is running before the wind in a rough sea. The stern rudder has replaced the side rudder, the aftercastle is more massive than in earlier ships, and dominates the forecastle. It contains accommodation for the master and officers and provides a more spacious deck above for warding off pirates. This ship anticipates the cog of the late fourteenth century.

The double-ended ships in which William the Conqueror invaded England in 1066; his flagship, her mast surmounted by his personal standard, is on the extreme right.

4   5   6

An interpretation of the two-masted cog, from a miniature in a fifteenth-century Florentine manuscript. Impressions of the cog or coque are numerous and differ greatly. It is probable that this ship carried a spritsail on the bowsprit. Her date would be late fourteenth or early fifteenth century.

Detail from the twelfth-century Belgian font in Winchester Cathedral showing what many authorities believe to be the first stern rudder.

become the upper control top of early steam-driven warships. The castles were a product of the Crusades. They were, for example, in evidence when Richard the Lion Heart of England sailed from Dartmouth in Devon in 1189 with a fleet of one hundred and fifty ships, bound for the Third Crusade. Castles first appeared in ships as temporary structures but by the end of the fifteenth century had become a permanent feature.

Of all centuries of ship design, the fifteenth produced a superabundance of ideas. Modifications to hulls, superstructure, rigging and improved sailing qualities prepared the way for the full-rigged ship, and so set in motion the age of discovery and exploration that was one of the great achievements of the Renaissance. The mariner of 1400 with a single mast and one sail to his ship would have been aston-

The carrack, an earlier relation of the galleon. This three-masted example dates from 1542. The long and graceful bowsprit and extension, and the twin rows of gun ports are interesting features. The ship has a characteristic deep sheer (fore-and-aft curvature) and was built in Genoa.

A model of a late fourteenth-century English cog, with characteristic rounded bows and deep hull. The Hansa cog was by contrast straight-ended, the lines of bow and stern from peak to keel being as straight as a ruler.

ished to see the three-masted ship of 1500 with her five or six sails and elaborate superstructure and rigging. Unhappily, the extent and variety of the changes were so scrappily documented and illustrated that it is not uncommon to come across three or more differing impressions of one particular ship. For example, it is impossible to reproduce with certainty a replica of Christopher Columbus's famous *Santa Maria*. All that can be said with conviction is that she belonged to a breed of ship known in Spain and Portugal as the *nao* (itself a word meaning, simply, a ship).

A breakaway in northern Europe from the centuries-old design of the single-masted ship brought the two-masted *cog*. As a cargo carrier she traded to the Mediterranean where her square sails and good sea-keeping qualities, added to easily handled rigging and an 'ample belly for money-making cargo', impressed Mediterranean traders. The Arab two-masted lateen rig that had served those traders so well gradually gave way to the new rig; and before many years had passed the two-masted ship was superseded by the three-master. Square sails were carried on the foremast and mainmast, and the third mast was called the mizzen. The sail it carried, an adaptation of

the lateen sail, was given the name of a 'fore-and-aft' sail; this ran parallel with the line of the ship from bow to stern. A square sail set, in contrast, across or athwart a ship's mast was known as 'square-rigged'.

The full-rigged ship had arrived. From this period, towards the end of the fifteenth century, the names given to different types of ship multiplied and can seem baffling today. The *carrack*, and its later relation the *galleon* were the true ancestors of the three-and four-masted full-rigged ships that were the backbone of sailing ship design for four centuries, until the coming of the steamship. The great *clippers* of the nineteenth century were a last refinement.

The ships of the late fifteenth and early sixteenth century that were employed in long oceanic voyages of discovery all stemmed from the carrack. By the standards of the day they were by no means prestige ships built for the glorification of monarchs but ordinary vessels, some so small that it is to be wondered they could be trusted to unknown seas. However, the achievements of the three-masted ship in the fifteenth century had nothing to do with size for size's sake. Its success lay in the quality and effectiveness of design of its masts, sails and rigging. These gave seamen a ship they could rely on to respond to

29

1. Columbus's *Santa Maria* was a type of ship known as a nao. This woodcut is a more realistic interpretation than many more elaborate colour impressions.

2. A galleon of the time of Queen Elizabeth I, with the Queen's standard at the foremast. The ship is straining at her anchor in a choppy sea.

3. English ships of the fourteenth century. Their permanent fore and aftercastles and side rudder follow with precision the ship pictured on the seal of Dover. An anchor, hove up, can be seen clearly on the ship in the foreground.

Oceanica Claffis

all shifts of weather and make distance in whatever direction the course lay. The ships of Columbus, Cabot and other discoverers of their time were less than a hundred feet in length – but they safely carried their navigators out and home.

Happily there were men of imagination with the means to act as patrons of seamanship. Prince Henry the Navigator was one of the great champions of the cause of the sea and ships. He was the younger son of King John I of Portugal; he was born in 1394, almost a century before Columbus's first voyage to the Americas. He founded a school of navigation at Sagres and sponsored voyages of discovery. Africa had a special fascination for him and many coastal ventures made towards West Africa and further south resulted in Sierra Leone being reached by 1460, the year of his death. Some historians point to Prince Henry as the first statesman to grasp that the great oceans were highways and not limitations to man's activities. His persistent enthusiasm and resources put Portugal fifty years ahead of more powerful European countries in oceanic exploration. Portugal was too small to hold her lead; but Prince Henry charted the way ahead. The Portuguese had evolved a ship type to which they gave the name *caravel*; its

A gallery of fifteenth-century shipbuilding in the Mediterranean, from Breydenbach's *Voyage to the Holy Land*.

1. A war galley making ready for sea, her decks covered with canvas to protect the workmen.

2. A single-masted ship: the main trunk of her mast has been stepped and the upper is ready for fitting; the next stage is rigging the ship.

3. A fully-framed carrack: the last sections of hull timber are being put into position.

4. A late fifteenth-century carrack under full sail; she closely resembles Columbus's nao, the *Santa Maria*.

5. A two-masted ship (early fifteenth century) with lateen rig and fore and aftercastles. The anchor has been cat-headed to the hull. The heavy boom at the stern could be interpreted as a precautionary aid to steering should the stern rudder be damaged.

The emergence of the full-rigged sailing ship: these drawings of sailing ships, as they developed in the most productive period in the history of their design from about 1400–1520, are based on a variety of contemporary impressions. In brief, they take the sailing ship from the simple, basically single-masted rig suitable for short-sea and coast-hugging voyages to the full-rigged ship that was capable of navigating vast stretches of ocean.

1. An early fifteenth-century ship with mainmast and primitive mizzen mast.

2. A ship of the later fifteenth century, about AD 1460. The underwater hull design shows little change; but in superstructure and rigging she has developed an extra deck, and the addition of a foremast.

1   2   3

ancestor was a lateen-rigged fishing boat, the caravela. It was the caravel, still lateen-rigged, that in Prince Henry's time sailed south along the coast of West Africa.

The seamen and explorers who were born within the circle of Europe in the fifteenth century could not help but imagine themselves at the centre of the world, however much they felt impelled to put to sea in search of other worlds and in order to confound the complacency of people who were content to believe, among other things, that the earth was flat. Beyond hearsay from fellow mariners they had little to go on, for the printed word was only then beginning to be available at all and then in dozens of copies rather than in thousands.

Shipwrights who designed ships and the seamen who sailed them were, quite rightly, as much concerned to develop their skills as were the merchant shipowners to make a profit. When they were looking to their hulls, rigs and tackle, and their sea horizons, there were other Europeans crossing thousands of miles of unmapped land and bringing back impressions of peoples and countries with seaboards and ships. Initially their impressions could be communicated only by word of mouth. Once printing had

extended communication and knowledge, the work of all travellers was more widely reported.

Ships as long-distance vehicles were perfected within the span of 1450 to 1500. This was also about the time when knowledge of the work of Marco Polo, one of the great explorers, began to penetrate Europe. Marco Polo had great influence on European thinking about the extent of the world, and in particular on the outlook of the mariner and what he could hope to achieve.

Yet Marco Polo had travelled to the Far East in 1292, two hundred years before Columbus set sail. Nevertheless, even if it had been possible for Marco Polo's writings to be broadcast throughout Europe in 1300, the ships of the day would not have been capable of facing the challenge of distance. At the same time, however, ships in the west were not so advanced as some of the craft described by Marco Polo. In China he found trading ships with crews of three hundred men. The ships had four masts carrying sails, plus banks of oars and sweeps. They had cabins for sixty merchants and could carry six thousand bags of pepper. They were equipped with as many as ten small boats, for the purpose of carrying out anchors, for fishing, and for a variety of other

32

3. A move towards the full-rigged ship. Here is a carrack with a more highly developed foremast, and a jigger mast at the stern.

4. A Portuguese carrack of about 1490. The foremast has been fully extended. A characteristic of a carrack's foreward end was that the forecastle overlapped the bows.

5. A ship of the early sixteenth century. Often called a galleon, a term applied loosely to many four-masted ships of grandiose concept, this type derives from the work of the fifteenth-century shipwrights who produced the full-rigged ship. Notice how the topcastles extend successively from the mainmast to the fore and mizzen masts, providing additional positions for defence.

4

5

services. They had wooden subdivisions in the hull, and if one section of a hold let in water after a collision, other sections remained watertight. Here in 1300 in China were ships that anticipated the passenger cargo ship of today – with watertight bulkheads and lifeboats and separate cabins for passengers.

This is a good point to look briefly at what had been happening in another and greater area of ocean than the Atlantic – the Pacific. Here, no great land masses stand in the way, to cause changes in the direction of the prevailing winds. In the roaring forties the winds blow constantly from the west. Were this not so the navigational achievements of the Polynesian people would have been impossible.

There are stories of fanciful devices that enabled the Polynesians to make accurate landfalls after passages across thousands of miles of the Pacific. But if one is to judge by the achievements of other mariners, it was experience, observation and natural judgement that led them to their destinations, until in the course of time they came to learn how to construct charts and mark the positions of the stars, particularly the Pole star.

As their islands became over-populated the Polynesians and Melanesians, collectively the Maori

people, colonized other islands, principally New Zealand. They used a craft called a *tainui*. It consisted of two canoes joined by stout cross-beams supporting a central cabin. The tainui's sails were unlike any form of sail elsewhere in the world with the exception of New Guinea. These lofty and deep sails resembled giant claws shaped to catch the least breath of wind. Captain Cook in his Pacific voyages of discovery in the eighteenth century met with the tainui and noted its elegance, particularly the high, ornamented stern posts. Equally impressive was the Maori war canoe. From the trunks of the high Kauri pine trees the Maoris fashioned canoes between sixty-five and seventy feet in length, but no more than five feet in the beam. The grace of their design was almost at odds with their purpose; certainly they were far superior to the standard 'dug-out'.

To close this middle period in the story of the ship, there follow some examples of interesting craft, among many in the world, that were built according to the demands of their function and the geographical and climatic conditions in which they sailed. It is possible to examine great numbers of craft still performing useful work in all parts of the world. But to find accurate evidence of their ancestry is difficult,

The tainui, a remarkable twin-hulled ocean-going craft in which the Maori people crossed thousands of miles of the Pacific Ocean on voyages of migration. Strength, stability, commodious space for the colonists and their possessions, and huge claw-shaped sails to catch the wind, and twin paddles for steering were practical features. The ornamented stern posts add grace to the tainui.

A reconstruction of a Maori war canoe, between sixty-five and seventy feet in length and hewn from a single Kauri pine tree. These shallow-draught craft were only five feet wide; they were paddled by as many as thirty men on each side, with an inverted triangular sail amidships to add to their speed. Their stern posts, as can be seen, were intricately carved.

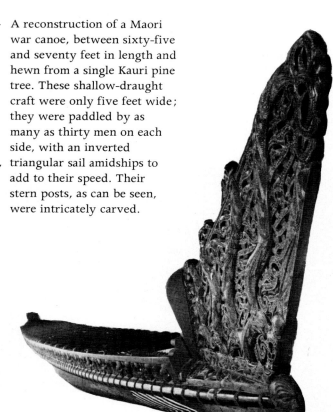

An inshore Hong Kong junk, a family houseboat as much a home as a means of earning a living. Shortness and great breadth, a single battened lugsail, and steering sweeps at bow and stern are characteristic of a craft that is now fast dying out.

The jangada, from Brazil —
more raft than boat (although
some have a semblance of a
deckhouse) — has probably
been in existence for six
thousand years.

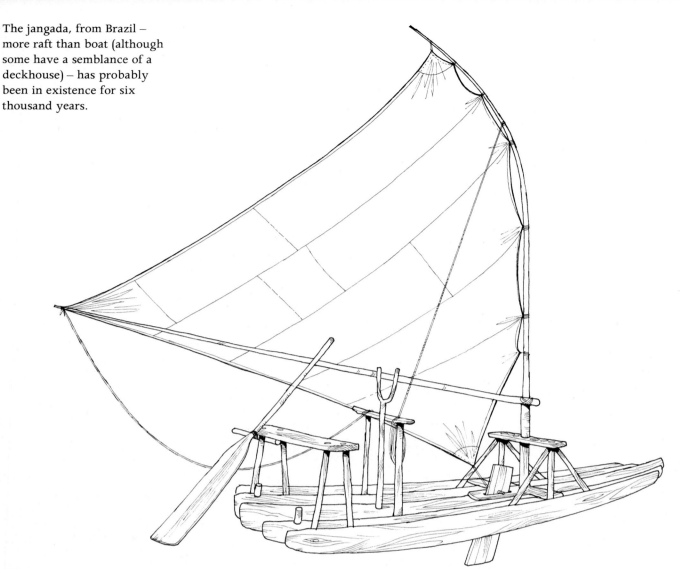

if indeed some of them had any ancestry. Native craft indigenous to a country can have shown little change over the centuries. Larger craft propelled by oars and sails will have been refined, some by influence of local custom, others by imported ideas. These small, ancient craft are the survivors of history.

The Patile of the River Ganges, India

The *patile* is a river cargo boat with a single mast and the lugsail common also to early Mediterranean trading ships. In appearance it resembles a houseboat because the hull is surmounted by a deckhouse thatched with palm leaves. On top is a catwalk for crew communication and for handling the sail and steering gear. But what gives the patile its originality are two other features: the hull is clinker built (with the planks overlapping) and is steered by a huge balanced side rudder: the latter is essential to manoeuvrability when the boat is full of cargo. Both these features are to be found in Viking ships, but it is out of the question that the Indian river sailors

used the principle of the clinker-built ship by communication with the Vikings. They must have discovered it independently — further evidence of peoples widely separated using their intelligence to reach similar conclusions.

The Irawadi Rice Boat, Burma

Here is a boat designed as the only speedy means of transporting goods and people in a country thick with impenetrable tropical jungle. Not only is the Irawadi *rice boat* a delight to look at, even something of a fairy-tale craft, but it continues to do useful work. Basically the hull is shaped as a dug-out. After it has been roughly fashioned it is then soaked to make it flexible and placed over a slow fire, when the fabric is stretched to its final form. The rig is original and delicately balanced to catch the southerly breezes of the Irawadi. Local artistry is reflected in the carved decorations of the stern. The rice boat makes no concessions to new-fangled stern rudders. It is steered by a side rudder, usually on the port side.

36

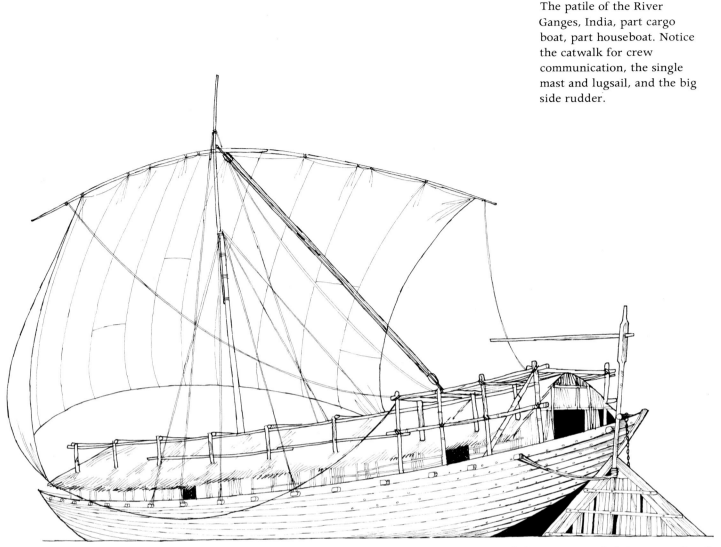

The Brazilian Jangada

In the first chapter we singled out the hobolo of Ethiopia, a craft confined to crossing to and fro on a little-known lake. In South America, Brazilians continue to employ a craft for fishing that is basically a raft, and can hardly have changed over thousands of years. Like the hobolo, this type of boat, so primitive in structure, seems to have little value or future in the twentieth century. But Björn Landström, the Swedish writer, who has devoted his life to the study of ships, suggests that the Brazilian *jangada* may yet outlive the nuclear-powered ship. The time difference between them could be six thousand years. It is, however, environment and purpose which determine the shape of ships.

The jangada, like the hobolo, uses a hull consisting of a number of logs of light wood. The single sail can be interpreted as a cross between a gaffsail and a spritsail. Some jangadas are more boat than raft in that they have a kind of deckhouse made out of reeds or thatch. To give stability to a sail-driven craft of such lightness the jangada has a form of keel: this is made of hardwood and extends downward from about amidships.

Two Portuguese Types

The Portuguese, who contributed greatly to the progress of ship design in the fifteenth century, were also inventive in adapting their coastal and river craft to local requirements. From this south-west corner of Europe two craft are especially notable. One, the *barco rabelo*, works the River Douro. The other, the *moliceiro*, is used on the lagoons of Aveiro. Both types have been in service for centuries.

The barco rabelo is a wine boat – and the only practical means of transporting casks of wine in the mountainous terrain that surrounds the River Douro, a swiftly flowing river broken by numerous rapids. To meet these conditions, and carry a worthwhile weight of cargo, centuries ago the Portuguese evolved this shallow-draught boat, shallow to float freely

A model of the Irawadi rice
boat, a Burmese river craft
still in use. Its striking
features include the elaborate
tackle on the mast, the
decorated deckhouse and the
side rudder; also the high
stern topped by a carved bird.

The decorated prow of a
Portuguese moliceiro: the boat
is common to the shallows
and lagoons of Aveiro.

A barco rabelo, the wine boat of the River Douro, Portugal, at moorings with a cargo of casks. The high trellis structure abaft the mast gives the helmsman control of the immensely long steering rudder.

high up the Douro, flexible in movement to negotiate the rapids. Wind and current carry the loaded boat down-stream, and she partly sails and is partly towed back. The barco rabelo averages sixty feet in length and can carry up to twenty-five tons of wine casks. She has an upswept bow, a flat stern, carries a single sail and is steered by a huge oar or sweep that resembles a stretched letter S. This sweep is more than thirty feet in length, which accounts for the ease with which the boat can be swung this way and that as she descends the rapids. The sail is fixed; the river is too narrow and difficult for tacking. If the wind drops after the barco rabelo has shot the rapids, the mast and yard are taken down and put over the side,

attached to the hull, to drift downstream with the boat.

The barco rabelo has a curious 'bridge', at least twelve feet high and of almost lattice-work construction; it needs to be high because the upper end of the steering oar projects well above the hull. The hull itself is interesting, being clinker built after the fashion of early Scandinavian ships.

The moliceiro is a boat so visibly fragile it seems she could scarcely be trusted to a pond. But in the conditions of shallow lagoons, undisturbed by more than a puff of wind, the moliceiro is as suited to her task as the most complex of today's ocean-going cargo carriers.

A Pacific outrigger with a
single claw-shaped sail
standing off the shore; a
merchant ship is at anchor in
the background.

The Moro outrigger, a canoe
still found in the Philippines.

A fully-loaded moliceiro in the shallows of a Portuguese lagoon. This boat has such a low freeboard that her deck amidships is no more than two or three inches above water.

In the illustration it can be seen that even the slightest of increases in deck load would submerge the moliceiro, so incredibly slight is her freeboard. Unchanged for centuries, the main purpose of the moliceiro is to harvest the water weed that thrives on the lagoons in the region of Aveiro and is a valuable manure for enriching the land.

Moro Fishing Boat, Southern Philippines

Our last example of strange craft is an outrigger canoe, the *moro*, still to be seen in Philippine fishing grounds. The outriggers are similar to those to be found throughout the Pacific; but the sail, seemingly big enough to make the craft airborne in a strong blow, is often splendidly colourful.

Three centuries of sail

A modern reconstruction of the *Mayflower*, a type of ship derived from the 'flute', in which the Pilgrim Fathers sailed in 1620.

Scilicet Octauo stupeant Miracula nostro
Ipsa, Tuúśq, operum, CAROLE, vincat apex.
Non patitur brutam Tellus ægerrima molem:
Hæc mouet, d́q habiles est animata molos.
Prona Semiramiam transportant Æquora turrim,
Et Mausolæum nat Tibi veluclum.
Numen in augustis Trabibus Geniale pererrat;
Fulmineos humilis pajsat ut Inda Lares!
Cernimus Aurato prætextam Vellere puppim;
Pilior est reduci Pasimelusa fide.
Labere cærulei pignus, sociale Tridentis,
Inter Deurantes una SVPREMA rates.
Nam Iouis Eléi Templum siluisse, fatendum:
En Neptunus in hac seruelat Arce Tonans.

Henr. Iacob

As we saw in the previous chapter, no other century in the long history of the sailing ship had produced such advances in design and sailing qualities as the fifteenth. Now, towards the end of the fifteenth century, Henry VII of England established himself as the first of the Tudors – a line that ruled the country during her most formative period overseas.

On becoming king, in 1485, he inherited a run-down shipping industry and a navy equally under-nourished, an example of the effects of civil war. The most, in fact, that can be said of the Wars of the Roses in the context of Britain's maritime affairs is that they brought about new thinking, better ships and also an urge to build big and elaborate ships for the sake of prestige. Certainly, the *prestige ship* was to become a national emblem, to be found in every generation of ships from the early 1500s to the present day.

In Scotland *c* 1511 the *Great Michael* was built. A carrack of 240 feet in length, she may have impressed the people but she offended a Scottish historian quoted by John Charnock in his *History of Marine Architecture:* 'She was of so great stature and took so much timber, that she wasted all the woods of Fife which were oak wood'. And in the Mediterranean there was built for the Knights of Malta a carrack as imposing as the *Great Michael*, called the *Santa Anna*.

Henry VII's shrewd business sense recognized that given the right kind of ships he could establish control of the seas without committing his exchequer to building and maintaining a navy. Henry VII was a man at the crossroads. He restored much of his country's wealth in the sea trades; built the required prestige ship, the *Regent*, and bequeathed to Henry VIII the economic problems of advancing British supremacy at sea and keeping open her trade routes. These considerations were further complicated by news from abroad of the successful voyages of discovery carried out by mariners such as Christopher Columbus, Vasco da Gama and Ferdinand Magellan.

Meanwhile the offensive power and size of the gun

had reached a stage at which a marine version could be installed below the upper decks of a ship. To fire a broadside the hull of a ship had to be pierced with gun ports. Their inventor was a M. Descharges, a French shipwright who lived in Brest.

In the period of change, invention, discovery and the early colonization of western territories overseas, new disciplines had to be applied to ship design. As in architecture, experience in the design and construction of ships created a breed of craftsmen – the master shipwrights. From the practice of fashioning

PEÑON DE VELES.

3. The *Ark Royal*, Lord Howard's flagship at the battle of the Armada, 1588.

4. The crescent formation of the Spanish Armada (right): this was preserved until fireships descended upon the fleet at Calais.

a hull by eye, relying on inherited flair, there developed the precision of the 'draught', or drawing of a ship's lines that was to become the blueprint of the naval architect.

Henry VIII showed an ardent interest in ships. In 1512 Sir Edward Howard was given charge of the King's ships. Dockyards were built on the Thames at Woolwich and Deptford and the Portsmouth establishment was strengthened. Henry persuaded the best shipwrights of Genoa and Venice to join his own technical corps. Inevitably he built a big ship, the *Henry Grâce à Dieu*, or 'Great Harry' as she was popularly named. She was built in 1514, but a complete refit in 1539 so altered her appearance that no reliance can be placed on the many impressions published in her time. As a fighting ship she was a liability, burdened with the top hamper of her castle-like superstructure.

By 1550 in northern Europe the sailing ship, either as a combatant or as a trading vessel, had been accepted. But in the Mediterranean there was support for a compromise vessel, the *galleass*, an attempt to combine the manoeuvrability of oars and the thrust of sails. In 1571, at the Battle of Lepanto, the last great sea fight between man-powered ships, the galleass routed the galley. However, it became generally recognized at this time that the ship relying solely on sail was the only vessel capable of long ocean voyages in a dual role of trading ship and man-of-war.

Elizabeth I's part in ship history was dominated by the seafaring genius of her captains, Drake, Frobisher, Hawkins and Howard, and by the triumph over the Spanish Armada. In Hawkins, Treasurer of the Queen Majesty's Marine Cause, Elizabeth had appointed a man, already an experienced deep-sea

3

4

The *Henry Grâce à Dieu*, or
'Great Harry', Henry VIII's
prestige ship, built in 1514.

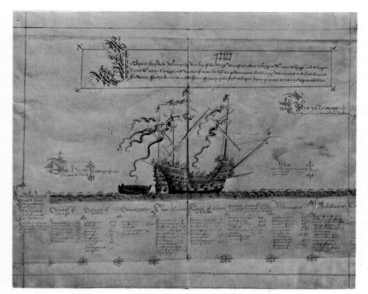

voyager, who had the administrative talent to limit and control the corrupt practices of the naval dockyards. Hawkins, Drake, and later Sir Walter Raleigh, having the skill of the shipwrights at their disposal, laid down the first of the fast, heavily gunned men-of-war that were to become *ships-of-the-line*. Drake's flagship at the Armada, the *Revenge*, of 300 tons, was a model for the future.

There is no doubting the devotion, and the astuteness, that the Tudors brought to their dealings with ships and the sea. One of the great shipwrights of Elizabeth's reign was Matthew Baker, who, in 1572, was made England's first master-shipwright. His father, James Baker, had been well known to Henry VIII, who granted him fourpence a day 'wage and fee'. Matthew Baker established a method to measure the tonnage of ships by working out the number of Bordeaux casks that could be stowed in the holds, a rule that was generally applied during his lifetime.

Towards the end of the sixteenth century, England still had no Royal Navy as an *exclusive* fighting force. There was not enough money to build, equip and maintain a permanent fleet. Commerce had to continue and the trading ships sparingly armed themselves with as small a sacrifice as possible of revenue-earning cargo space. In the face of piracy, merchant shipowners grouped themselves together

in self-defence to form the first shipping company or shipping line. In this way the East India Company began and the trading ship, or more properly the merchant ship, became known as an Indiaman.

While attention was lavished on prestige ships, which were costly to build and run, there was quiet progress in Holland in the design of small, unspectacular ships; these were also proving a commercial success. Their rig was simple, they required few men to sail them, and they made substantial profits for their Dutch owners, who rapidly secured a lead in the European carrying trades. Typical of these ships was the *fluyt*, sometimes spelt *flute*, and known in English as the *flyboat*. Of the same family was the *Mayflower*, in which the Pilgrim Fathers sailed to America in 1620. She was no more than 120 tons.

At the other end of the scale there was the continuing obsession of monarchs to build big ships. In 1610 James I built the *Prince Royal* at Woolwich. Within ten years of each other Gustavus Adolphus of Sweden and Charles I of England built the *Vasa* and the *Sovereign of the Seas*, ships with very different fates. The *Sovereign of the Seas* (1637) was the largest ship in the world. She was a showpiece, built without any thought of a budget and encrusted with elaborate decoration and carving. She carried 100 guns on three decks and was so much ahead of her time that she could have fought at Trafalgar. Ships of this character invoke impressive statistics, but lengths and breadths and depths convey nothing of the majesty of the *Sovereign of the Seas*.

Contemporary pictures reveal her for what she was, an extravagant whim of Charles I. Ships of this period had long lives; they were altered and sometimes completely rebuilt. As Lord Protector, Oliver Cromwell's Puritan instincts caused him to abhor Charles I's excesses in design and embellishment, and he had the *Sovereign of the Seas* cut down to his ideas by removing all carvings and decoration and by altering and reducing her rig. The *Sovereign of the Seas* survived for nearly sixty years, but she was a very different ship when, in 1696, a candle, acciden-

James Cook's flagship *Resolution*, in which he penetrated further south into the Antarctic than any other explorer. In the background is the *Discovery*.

The Thames barge, a river and coastal craft now centuries old but still at work, largely unnoticed on a river crammed with ships having every possible navigational aid at their disposal.

An impression of the *Vasa*, based on the restored hull, as she appeared when she left Stockholm on her maiden voyage in 1628; she sank within hours of departure.

tally overturned, caused a fire that destroyed her.

Her near contemporary, the *Vasa* of Sweden, was much the same size, 170 feet in length, but much narrower in the beam at less than forty feet. Her draught, little more than fourteen feet, was five feet shallower than the *Sovereign of the Seas*. A ship of these dimensions, fully rigged and equipped with an armament of forty-eight twenty-four-pounder guns, many of them placed high in the superstructure, sacrificed stability. The guns alone weighed eighty tons. Preparations for the *Vasa's* maiden departure from Stockholm were elaborate.

When the *Vasa* raised sail on 10 August 1628, thousands were there to see the great ship towed

from her berth into mid-stream to begin the forty-mile trip to the open sea. She had on board 450 men, 150 seamen and 300 military personnel. By special dispensation they had been allowed to take their families as far as the outer reaches of the harbour. Clear of the headlands, the *Vasa's* sails caught the wind and she began to make headway. Moments later she began to heel alarmingly; water rushed in through the lower gun ports and gradually the *Vasa* disappeared. She righted herself as she went down. Most of her ship's company and their families were above decks and were picked up by harbour craft, so that the loss of life was no more than fifty.

If the *Vasa* made a short and spectacular maiden

A sixteenth-century work after Pieter Brueghel the Elder, showing carracks in harbour.

A model of an unnamed Elizabethan galleon *c* 1600. Obviously based on Drake's successful *Revenge*, this ship is entirely functional while being well-balanced in design. The absence of elaborate carving and decoration is noticeable.

voyage, she sank so evenly and gently in a hundred feet of water that her hull rested upright on the sandy bottom. Three hundred and thirty-three years later, in April 1961, the hull of the *Vasa* was brought to the surface, cradled by pontoons, after a salvage operation that had been thought of, abandoned as impossible and revived when the techniques of ship raising, used painstakingly at Scapa Flow to bring up the steel battleships of Germany's scuttled fleet from the First World War, proved that with careful planning even a fragile wooden hull could be surfaced. Today the *Vasa* rests in a permanent berth in a Stockholm drydock, the most perfectly preserved ship of the seventeenth century.

In the midst of these spectacular ventures with big sailing ships, one of many small sailing craft has survived for centuries. The Thames barge deservedly has a place in history. In the Great Plague of London in 1665, Thames barges from Ware, were the only boats that carried provisions to the city. In rig and design the Thames barge remained unchanged for centuries, with a large spritsail, a topsail, and two, sometimes three, headsails. Most important was the small mizzen sail placed right aft, not to give speed but to help the helmsman haul the big rudder over. The sail was sheeted down to the edge of the rudder. This was practical and economical, for the Thames barge carried a crew of only two men and a boy.

The shipwright who supervised the building of the *Sovereign of the Seas* was Phineas Pett, one of a family that became known throughout Europe in the seventeenth century. Opinions about Phineas are divided. It has been said that he was a copyist; Samuel Pepys, for one, had little respect for him.

The fame of Pepy's diary has tended to obscure his work for the British navy. But in his time as Secretary of the Admiralty, during the Restoration, a fleet of ships was financed and created solely as a sea-going fighting force. Also during this period, battle tactics were radically changed. Instead of warships meeting the enemy in an uncoordinated assault they deployed in line ahead, that is, one behind the other. Hence the 'ship-of-the-line', signifying a ship of sufficient gun power to merit a position in the van of a sea battle.

Pepys had a high regard for Sir Anthony Deane, the great naval architect, who, with Matthew Baker, brought the sailing ship to a standard that was not matched until the slim-lined clippers of the nineteenth century. Deane wrote a classic study of ship design in 1670 called *The Doctrine of Naval Architecture*. The book was written at the instigation of Pepys, who esteemed it so highly that he showed a copy to his fellow diarist John Evelyn in 1682, remarking: 'I esteem this book an extraordinary jewel'.

This ship, with almost all her sails gone, and her masts and rigging in disorder, shows vividly the conditions of winds and sea that captains of sailing ships had to accept.

Samuel Pepys, John Evelyn and Sir Anthony Deane dined together on 7 March 1690, a meeting recorded in Evelyn's diary. Deane pointed out the advantage Britain had in possessing frigates, the first country to do so, and mentioned the *Constant Warwick*, as 'a vessel that would sail swiftly, it was built with low decks, the guns lying near the water; and was so light and swift of sailing that in a short time she had taken as much money from privateers as would laden her'. Deane, as always, had pre-

science, for the design was brought to full efficiency in the next century.

Deane was well aware of the quality of foreign warship design. In fact, the French at that time were building much superior ships to the British. An outstanding example was the seventy-four-gun *Superbe*. Charles I and Deane visited her in 1672 and were so impressed that Deane measured her and subsequently incorporated her best features in British ships-of-the-line. In relation to her length the *Superbe* was

A Dutch merchant ship under half sail bearing down on a whale in a rough sea. (From a painting by Cornelisz Verbeek.)

Full-rigged ship approaching harbour, in a painting by Willem Van Der Velde the Younger (1633 – 1707). These late seventeenth-century Dutch ships are models of clean design.

much broader in the beam than earlier ships, and she had a deeper draught – both features that made her a steadier gun platform. She has only to be compared with the *Vasa* to prove the point.

At this stage, it is worthwhile considering the demands that wooden ships made on supplies of timber. To build one ship of 1,370 tons needed 2,000 oak trees. Where timber had been used without thought, forests were being depleted at an alarming rate, and further uses had to be found for iron. Ship-wrights began to use iron to connect the beams of a ship to her hull. An example was the sixty-four-gun ship-of-the-line *Agamemnon*, built at Buckler's Hard on the Beaulieu River in 1781. Some 100 tons of wrought iron were used inside the ship, and thirty tons of copper sheathed the hull. The *Agamemnon* was eighteen months in building; she later became one of Nelson's favourite commands.

In the Mediterranean, Barbary State pirates continued to prey on merchant shipping. Speed, ease

In 1609, eleven years before the *Mayflower* sailed from Plymouth, merchants were advertising the merits of the *Nova Britannia* and the advantages of life in Virginia.

Mediterranean galleys persisted in the Mediterranean, even after their decisive defeat at the Battle of Lepanto in 1571. This group of bizarre ships (late sixteenth century), each with a differently designed aftercastle, shows the great breadth of these craft, the immense lateen yards and banks of rowers, four and five men to an oar.

NOVA BRITANNIA.

OFFERING MOST

Excellent fruites by Planting in VIRGINIA.

Exciting all such as be well affected to further the same.

LONDON
Printed for SAMVEL MACHAM, and are to be sold at his Shop in Pauls Church-yard, at the Signe of the Bul-head.
1609.

of handling and fire power were essential. The craft that pirates refined was the *xebec* or *chebeck*, a throwback employing the lateen sail of the dhow. Nine oars to each side perpetuated the principle of the galley, now outpaced as a fighting ship by the ship-of-the-line, but a valuable and cheap-to-build instrument of piracy. A typical xebec was armed with sixteen guns, fired through holes in the bulwarks.

On the far side of the western ocean, the Caribbean was also swarming with pirates. In their inter-island traffic and voyages up and down the eastern American seaboard, the colonists had devised small, swift ships that could outpace their enemies. Some marine historians, although not claiming that the Americans invented the fast sailer, think it likely that the environment before and during the War of Independence gave boat builders and shipmasters alike a taste for speed, which, within fifty years, produced the clipper ship.

Pirates and corsairs were damned as the villains of the sea, but privateers were strangely held to be respectable, whereas in reality there was little to choose between them. Privateering was a euphemism to salve the consciences of kings and queens, and also those of the wealthy gentry who pooled their resources to build and man privateers. In fact the crown benefited; in 1550 Edward VI gained revenue from the licences he issued entitling the bearer to capture ships and their lucrative cargoes. Elizabeth I was as much an opportunist as Sir Francis Drake and encouraged and partly financed privateering ventures. Most remarkable was the capture in 1592 of the Spanish treasure ship *Madre de Dios*, intercepted when she had almost reached home. A British squadron took possession of the ship to discover that the value of her cargo of precious stones, pearls and gold ornaments was no less than £2,500,000.

From piracy to smuggling – (an activity that still flourishes) and so to the *cutter* – a popular craft around the coast of Britain in the late eighteenth century. Some of the North Sea cutters of 130 tons were powerfully armed, with up to seventeen guns and a crew of forty. In 1783, to take a single example, the cutter *Swift* crept into Torbay in Devon with

Phineas Pett, one of a famous family of shipwrights, was born in Deptford in 1570 and followed Matthew Baker as Master of the Shipwrights' Company in 1607; he was responsible to Charles I for the design and construction of the *Sovereign of the Seas*.

Sir Anthony Deane (1638 – 1721), one of the greatest of ship designers, whose practical and written contributions to the art and science of shipbuilding were immeasurable. He won the confidence of Charles II, later that of James II; Samuel Pepys admired him for his talent and was also his close friend.

2,000 casks of spirits and five tons of tea, a cargo that was brought ashore in next to no time by a party of 200 enthusiastic beneficiaries of the enterprise.

The big ocean-going trading ship continued to be called an East Indiaman, wherever she was built. In Sweden an East India Company was formed in 1731. In common with the British East India Company their ship designers were obliged to make compromises to provide both cargo space and an armament of war-ship weight for defence against pirates. Of the Swedish merchant ships of the late eighteenth century the *Götheborg*, built in 1786, makes an interesting comparison with an English version, the *True Britain*, which disappeared on a voyage between Bombay and China in 1809.

There is a fascination about these ships. The British East India Company grew to a level of such wealth and influence that the fortunes and fringe benefits of its captains became legendary. An East Indiaman's captain had a basic pay of £10 a month. But the passage money paid by passengers went into his own pocket. He had a share in the profits on cargo, and often carried freight to his own private benefit. Accounts of East India captains making £6,000 in one voyage are quite believable.

For passengers in an East Indiaman, life was no picnic. A so-called first-class cabin measured seven feet by six; for this an officer of colonel's rank paid £250 for a passage to China. Not-so-important passengers occupied the 'tween-decks, where the only concessions to privacy were canvas screens. When an enemy or a pirate was sighted, the screens were whipped away, the guns run out and the Indiaman became a man-of-war, the unfortunate passengers finding what shelter they could. Because they were hybrids, combining the weight of considerable cargo with the burden of heavy guns, with passengers thrown in as makeweight, East Indiamen were possibly the most sluggish ships ever built. A Captain Basil Hall, RN, was caustic about their sailing qualities: 'In a calm they drifted about like logs of wood and the progress of one haystack of a vessel was so slow that a fast sailing ship was directed to take her in tow.' For all that, the East India Company in 250

1. A lively painting that highlights the dangers of whale-grappling in a small boat.

2. British and American whaling ships off the Cape of Good Hope in the early nineteenth century – Table Mountain can be seen in the background. Notice the Stars and Stripes flying from a lance in the whale in the foreground. (After a lithograph by Lebreton.)

3. Dutch whaling ships in the Arctic in 1791. Whales were slaughtered in massive quantities: during the season as many as a thousand ships called at Spitzbergen, headquarters of the northern whaling fleets.

1

3

2

The *Agamemnon*: one of Nelson's favourite commands in the Mediterranean, this ship was built in 1781. Shipyards were by then growing concerned about vanishing timber resources, and more and more applications were found for metal. The *Agamemnon* used a hundred tons of wrought iron inside her hull, which was sheathed in thirty tons of copper.

The *True Britain*, an East Indiaman built in 1790; in 1809 she disappeared on a voyage between Bombay and China.

years won great commercial and political power in India and China. It even had its own army.

Whaling was, and still is, a hazardous industry. Hazardous in the early days when ships, mainly Dutch, penetrated the Arctic on voyages of indeterminate length that were completed when the last ton of blubber left just enough space for the hatches to be battened down. They were ships commanded by men with the ability to tame their hard-case crews – men who lived rough only for their share of the profits from the slaughter of whales.

The base of the northern whaling fleets was Spitzbergen, where the Dutch had their own headquarters that they named *Smeerenberg*, or 'Blubbertown'. In an eighteenth-century Arctic whaling season as many as a thousand ships would call at Spitzbergen. Exploitation on this scale so reduced the whale population that it was indeed ironic that Captain James Cook's voyage of discovery to Australia, and towards Antarctica, should have revealed so great a reserve of whales and seals that the fleets of whaling ships were glutted with meat and blubber within days of their arrival in the whaling grounds.

Alan Moorehead in *The Fatal Impact* describes the rape of Antarctic wild life that followed in the trail of the dedicated explorers, men of the character of Cook who charted the southern seas and wrote in their journals and logs detailed descriptions of the wonders they had seen. Moorehead obviously could not put an accurate figure to the number of whales killed in Antarctica in the fifty years after Cook's voyages, but he mentions that it could have been anywhere between ten and fifty million. Whaling was a dangerous calling: whales of the size, endurance and destructive power of Melville's *Moby Dick* were not figments of imagination. And they had to be fought from a rowing boat. The boat had to come close enough to put the harpooner in a position to secure a hit; the crew then attacked the whale with lances, at the same time keeping the boat clear of the whale's wildly thrashing tail. Often a right whale would take charge of the boat and tow it for miles; on the other hand, a sperm whale's reaction to attack was a deep dive, and the harpooner who neglected to sever the towline at the correct moment would take boat and crew into the depths. Whaling tactics continued in this way until a Norwegian, Svend Foyn, invented the grenade harpoon in 1864. With this device a whaling boat could stand off its prey; the harpooner fired his gun, the grenade penetrated the body of the whale and exploded.

Whaling ships and slave ships may at first seem strange companions. But on different oceans they advanced the design of ships for special purposes. As early as the sixteenth century, in their explorations of the American continent, the Spaniards

A model of a three-masted lateen-rigged xebec (or chebeck), the principal assault ship of Mediterranean pirates in the eighteenth and nineteenth centuries.

The slaver *L'Antonio*, a rakish, fast-sailing craft that sped with the trade winds from West Africa to the southern states of the USA, carrying hundreds of slaves. In hull form and rig she anticipates the Baltimore clippers of the early nineteenth century.

decided that the native Indians were unfitted for disciplined labour; so, gradually but persistently, the slave trade from West Africa developed. The ocean route to the Americas was climatically kind, and the south-east trade winds were favourable for fast passages. From the slow and sluggish successors to the English round ships grew the swift schooners and brigs that carried African slaves in unspeakably crowded and squalid conditions. But the mortality rate was now lower because the ocean passage was faster.

In the year 1771 British ships brought 47,000 slaves to South Carolina and Virginia. By then American ships also had a footing in the trade, which reached such proportions that Congress passed an act on 22 March 1794 to prevent ships being built as slavers. Even so there were enough unscrupulous traders prepared to risk forfeiture of their ships.

As the eighteenth century was ending, the clippers were in embryo. Great changes were in prospect

58

– in sail and steam. Before the War of Independence American ship designers had learned the craft of shipbuilding from Europe, and, as has been seen, they had the incentives to go on and produce the utmost speed from a sail-driven hull. It is no accident that, when the trading sailing ship disappeared from the seas, American devotees of sail produced a new breed of craft, the sleek yachts that over the years have competed so successfully in the races for the America's Cup, outsailing all opposition.

A comment from Howard I. Chapelle, the American marine historian, exactly sums up the mystery and fascination of the story of sail. This is a passage from his classic study, *The Search for Speed Under Sail*. 'It must be remembered that ships themselves are the best and most common means of conveying information on their design to a foreign area. The copying process thus began in ancient times – hundreds of years before ship design records are available. It is quite impossible to determine how much real knowledge existed as to the design of fast sailing vessels at any given time before 1690. But there is some evidence that we have underestimated the knowledge of ship designers prior to 1800. How much of their knowledge can be credited to their inspection of foreign vessels is an unanswered question.'

The clipper ship

The *Archibald Russell* under full sail. She was one of the last of the steel-built sailing ships constructed at the shipyard of Scotts at Greenock, in 1905.

Donald McKay's famous clipper *Flying Cloud* (1851): she covered the run from New York to San Francisco in eighty-nine days, a record that was never surpassed and proof of McKay's mastery of ship design.

The British *Anglesey* (1852), one of the Blackwall frigates built in the early 1850s, so named because many of the class were built at Blackwall on the Thames. She was a ship of 965 tons and had a length of 182 feet.

The *Challenge* (1851) designed by William H. Webb; at 2,006 tons she was one of the largest clippers afloat. Her most famous commander was Captain Waterman, who had made record passages in the *Sea Witch*.

Sail plan of a clipper, the great American ship *Flying Cloud* of 1851. This drawing is from the lee-side of the ship; it shows how her sails are filling to the wind from the port side. The sleekness of the hull design and the practical precision of the sail plan reveal that 'extreme' clippers, as they were called, demanded absolute skill in handling and in seamanship. She is fully-rigged on foremast, mainmast and mizzen mast.

1 Outer jib
2 Inner jib
3 Fore topmast staysail
4 Lower studding sail (brailed up behind jibs)
5 Fore topmast studding sail
6 Fore topgallant studding sail
7 Fore royal studding sail
8 Fore sail or fore course
9 Fore topsail
10 Fore topgallant sail
11 Fore royal sail
12 Fore skysail
13 Main topmast staysail
14 Main topgallant staysail
15 Main royal staysail
16 Main sail or main course
17 Main topsail
18 Main topgallant sail
19 Main royal sail

The end of Napoleon's domination of Europe, in 1815, and the settlement of peace between Britain and the United States after the war of 1812 – 14, were events that in both countries renewed the zest to build sailing ships.

Before the century was over sailing ship design and performance were to reach their limits. In the earlier part of the nineteenth century the fast American *Baltimore packets*, and later the *clippers*, held the lead. The packets and clippers showed a clean pair of heels to the early steamships. There was in this period, often called the golden age of sail, an instinctive sense that the sailing ship, as a trader and as a warship, was entering a final phase and this – almost in defiance of the steamship – impelled designers to produce their best work.

The Baltimore packet ships were the predecessors of the clipper ships; and the design of the packets can be traced to the swift French *luggers* that traded in

American waters during the war with England in 1812.

In Britain in 1815 the East India Company still held sway and its ships in principle had not altered for more than a century. The packet ship came on the scene in 1816, and the clipper ship era in America covered the period from 1845 to the opening of the Suez Canal in 1869. Its best years lie between 1845 and 1855. The British clippers, their design initially based on American models, developed rapidly from 1851 onwards. Design impetus was aided by the repeal of the British navigation laws and by the arrival in London in 1850 of the *Oriental*, the first American clipper to berth in the Thames docks. The twenty years that followed saw a succession of splendid ships, trading profitably in the Indian and China tea trades and in the Australian emigrant and cargo trade. Under the command of captains who were great seamen and masters of the craft of ship-handling they made remarkable passages.

20 Main skysail
21 Spanker, or driver
22 Cross-jack (brailed up)
23 Lower mizzen royal sail
24 Upper mizzen topsail
25 Mizzen topgallant sail
26 Mizzen royal sail

The *Lynx*, a Baltimore schooner of 1812. Her hull forward is not all that fine-lined, but towards the stern her form hints at the clippers to come. Simple in rig but designed for speed, the *Lynx* has something in common with the slave ship *L'Antonio* of the previous chapter.

There are those who dismiss 1816 to 1845 as stagnant years in ship design or at most a period when tough mates became even tougher captains intent on making fast passages whatever the cost in injured crews or torn sails and broken topmasts. On the contrary, they were productive years. More was learnt of the techniques of ship construction so that vessels could be built with greater efficiency; rigging was simplified and deck machinery was improved, all of which benefited subsequent clipper ship design.

What was the origin of the word clipper? Going 'at a good clip' is a familiar phrase today to denote speed. John Dryden used a version of the word in his poem *Annus Mirabilis*, written in 1667:

'Some falcon stoops at what her eye designed,
And, with her eagerness the quarry missed,
Straight flies at check, and clips it down the
wind.'

The first part of the poem deals with the sea and ships, describing three naval actions between the British and Dutch in 1665 and 1666; and 'clips it down the wind' is precisely what a clipper did. And because they had such fine lines and sharp hulls they were sensitive to light airs; in the hands of a talented captain they would ghost through smooth seas when heavier, bulkier ships lay becalmed.

First off the mark of the Atlantic or western ocean packet lines was the American Black Ball Line, which opened a service in 1816 between Liverpool and New York with four ships, each of 500 tons. They were named *Amity*, *Courier*, *Pacific* and *James Monroe*. The *Liverpool Courier*'s shipping correspondent wrote of the *Pacific*'s accommodation: 'Her dining room is 40 feet by 14. The end of the dining room is spanned by an elliptical arch, supported by handsome pillars of Egyptian porphery...' That was all very well. But once the space occupied by the dining

Possibly the greatest race between sailing ships ever: in 1866 the China clippers *Taeping* and *Ariel* race up the English Channel at the close of a contest which began 16,000 miles away in Foochow. In the end, after ninety-nine days at sea, the *Taeping* won by twenty minutes.

room and the fourteen first class cabins that led off it had been deducted from the ship's cubic capacity there was meagre accommodation for the emigrants whose passage money yielded the most profit on a voyage. Conditions were more than primitive. The emigrants were virtually stowed in the 'tween-decks. They had to bring their own food with them, fight to secure a place at the stoves to cook it, and spend the night on wooden shelves or trays – all this in a battened-down, heaving and pitching ship.

Ten similar ships made up the second generation of the Black Ball Line – easily recognizable at sea by the black ball displayed on the topsails. Their average length of passage from Liverpool to New York was thirty-three days; with the westerlies behind them they returned in twenty-two days. One ship did better than the others; the *Canada* reached Liverpool in fifteen days eighteen hours.

The arrivals of the packets at Liverpool were signalled to the Pier Head by flags on the top of Bidston Hill overlooking Liverpool Bay. The more prominent merchants each had their own flagpole. The British agents of the Black Ball Line were Cropper and Benson. When one of their ships was sighted off the Bar Light, fifteen miles from Liverpool, a flag with a black ball painted on it was hoisted so that preparations could be made to receive the ship.

James Cropper not only had a ship named after him, made a fortune from his Black Ball agency and a shipping line of his own, but took up the anti-slavery cause as a result of meeting Thomas Clarkson in 1816. Clarkson and William Wilberforce campaigned for the abolition of slave traffic, and after Wilberforce's death, in 1833, Clarkson and James Cropper continued to press for the outlawing of slave ships.

Events came crowding in during these years to

advance the design of the packet ships and the demand for their services. New York's trade, growing rapidly as emigrants and cargoes flowed in from Europe, was given a fillip by the opening of the Erie Canal in 1825, which enabled smaller ships with transhipped cargo to penetrate far deeper into the American hinterland.

In 1833 the British East India Company's contract was not renewed. Its monopoly of the Indian and Far Eastern trades came to an end, but British shipowners in these trades continued to employ the crews of East Indiamen, and did not depart from the design of the ships. An exception was Duncan Dunbar, an enigmatic man who lived from 1804 until 1862, never built a steamship but was so single-minded that he had no interests other than ships, and amassed a fortune of £1,500,000. He was impatient with the tediously long voyages of the East Indiamen – they shortened sail at night and, as it were, went to sleep – and he was impatient with the unreasonable length of time they spent in each port. While other British shipowners were content to bask under the protection of the Navigation Laws – for example they enjoyed the privilege that all imports from foreign countries should be carried in British ships – Dunbar went in for ships that were faster than the Indiamen, and he exhorted his captains to make quick turn-rounds in port, offering them bonuses to do so.

Dunbar introduced into his fleet ships that were known collectively as Blackwall frigates because most of the class were built at Blackwall on the Thames. But Dunbar, always a man to strike a bargain, had his ships built at Sunderland. His enterprise and initiative led him also to establish his own shipbuilding yard at Moulmein in Burma, where he built ships for himself and other owners at realistic costs. Ready to hand were unlimited supplies of teak, the best of the hard woods for shipbuilding; and local labour that, under supervision, was perfectly capable of constructing ships of the highest class.

When he was fifty-one, Dunbar had the largest privately owned merchant fleet in the world, total-ling 40,000 tons. He never married; ships came first, and, to use a colloquial phrase, he played things so close to the chest that he alone was the business. When he dropped dead in 1862 at the age of fifty-eight there was no one to carry on, and the great fleet that he had built up was sold piecemeal.

Ships and the sea, by nature unpredictable, bred a race of individualists. There were great discoverers and naval architects, and men who employed ships to make their fortunes. There were yet others who charted the oceans and the weather.

One such navigational genius, Lieutenant Matthew Fontaine Maury of the US Navy, delved into ships' log books, and the charts and records deposited in Washington in their thousands. These recorded the characters of oceans, currents and winds at all seasons of the year. In 1855, while Duncan Dunbar was making his fortune; while Samuel Cunard was building up what was to become the largest fleet of passenger liners on the North Atlantic, and while the clippers were approaching their zenith and Brunel was planning his great iron ship, the *Great Eastern*, Maury published his *Physical Geography of the Sea*. It became the shipmaster's bible. Long before the first Atlantic cable was laid, for instance, Maury had discovered that the sea bed between Ireland and Newfoundland formed 'a plateau which seems to have been placed there especially for the purpose of holding a submarine telegraph cable'.

And in 1855 Maury suggested that sea traffic on the Atlantic was growing so rapidly that a system of tracks should be drawn up. Ships sailing westbound would use one set of tracks; ships bound for Europe would follow a different set. Years later his proposal was accepted.

From men to ships. The first true clipper ship to be built in America was the *Rainbow,* launched in 1845 after delays caused by controversy and criticism from traditionalists. During her short life – the *Rainbow,* lost on her fifth voyage in 1848 while bound from New York to Valparaiso, is thought to have foundered off Cape Horn – she made a fast passage from New York to China in ninety-two days, returning in eighty-eight days by way of the Cape of Good Hope. The performance of the *Rainbow* silenced the doubters and so impressed her owners and her critics that a second ship was laid down, and launched as the *Sea Witch* in 1846. *Sea Witch,* one of the fastest of the clippers, made her maiden voyage in the China trade. Her best day's run was 358 miles at fifteen knots, a speed that no steamship of the time could touch. But no clipper could reach and maintain that kind of progress for weeks on end unless she was in capable hands. Clipper captains piled on sail until the lee rail was under water. They were strict disciplinarians, especially the more talented masters, who regarded seamanship as an art. They drove their crews hard and sent them aloft in wild weather, not to reduce sail, but to set royals.

A captain could make or break a clipper. She would respond to skill as a thoroughbred horse obeys the least touch of rein. Joseph Conrad writes of a clipper captain who lost his nerve, charging through a line of ships at anchor, one of which he narrowly missed ramming. 'Afterwards the master said to me in a shy mumble, "She wouldn't luff up in time, somehow. What's the matter with her?" And I made no answer. Yet the answer was clear. The ship had found out the momentary weakness of her man. Of all the living creatures upon land and sea, it is ships alone that cannot be taken in by barren pretences, that will not put up with bad art from their masters.'

At the end of the 1840s two events occurred that brought the clippers into their own and made them undisputed masters of all passenger and cargo ships. The British Navigation Laws were repealed in 1849 and the way was opened for American clippers to carry cargoes of tea to Britain. The first ship to arrive in London was the *Oriental* with 1,600 tons of tea. She moored in the West India Docks in December 1850 after a voyage of ninety-seven days from Hong Kong, and immediately became a centre of attention, for few Londers had set eyes on a clipper ship. When one considers that the freight money was £9,600 and

that the first cost of the *Oriental* was £14,000 it is not difficult to see that her owners were in for tremendous profits. Obviously, British tea merchants gave their business to the American clippers. True, they had to pay higher freight rates for the speed, but they were more than compensated by regular arrivals and by the better condition of the tea after a shorter voyage. British shipowners reacted sharply by building ships to the American pattern. In the late 1850s there was a slump in American shipping and it was then that the British clippers came to the forefront.

In 1848 vast gold strikes had been discovered in California that drew people from all over the world, madly anxious to stake their claims. In 1849 alone, 91,405 passengers arrived at San Francisco. There were extraordinary scenes. Complete crews, captains, officers and men deserted their ships and made for the gold mines. Every conceivable type of ship was diverted from her regular route to brave the storms of Cape Horn and carry passengers to California. Passenger and freight rates rose to levels that justified shipowners sending their ships empty from San Francisco to China to load a cargo of tea for London. Clipper shipbuilding in America reached its zenith in 1853, when no fewer than forty-eight ships were completed for the Californian trade.

Round-the-world voyages became commonplace, as also did record voyages and unofficial races. The *Sea Witch* entered San Francisco on 24 July 1850 after a record ninety-seven days from New York that included weathering Cape Horn in the middle of the southern winter. On another occasion, in 1851, the *Sea Witch* took part in a race from Boston to San Francisco, her contestants being the *Raven* and *Typhoon.* All three ships left within days of each other.

The precision of their captains and crews is proven by the closeness of their performances. *Raven* was first in 105 days; *Typhoon* was placed second in 106 days and *Sea Witch* (not in her usual form) was third in 110 days. Another impressive ship, the *Flying Cloud,* covered the run from New York to San Fran-

Donald McKay's masterpiece, the *Great Republic,* as originally rigged in 1853. She was the largest wooden sailing ship ever built.

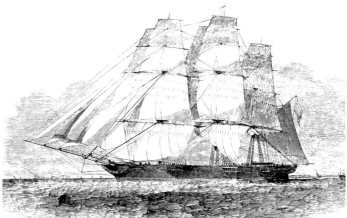

The American clipper *Oriental,* the first to dock in London (1850). She carried the first tea cargo to the Thames under the American flag after the repeal of the British Navigation Laws.

cisco in eighty-nine days, a record equalled but never surpassed (later the *Flying Cloud* herself repeated the performance).

An extract from the *Flying Cloud's* log is revealing, not so much for the weather and sail changes but for the unexpected happenings: 'Very severe thunder and lightning, double-reefed topsails, split main topmast stay sails. At 1 pm discovered mainmast had sprung, sent down royal and topgallant yards and studding sail booms off lower and topsail yards to relieve strain – July 13th. Let men out of irons in consequence of wanting their services, with the understanding that they would be taken care of on arriving at San Francisco. At 6 pm carried away the main topsail tye and band round the mainmast – July 23rd. Cape Horn north five miles. The whole coast covered with snow – July 31st. Fresh breezes, fine weather, all sail set. At 2 pm, wind southeast. At 6 squally; in lower and topgallant studding sails; 7, in royals; at 2 am in foretopmast studding sail. Latter part, strong gales and high sea running. Ship very wet fore and aft. Distance this day by observation is 374 miles. During the squalls 18 knots of line was not sufficient to measure the speed. Topgallant sails set – August 3rd. At 3 pm suspended first officer from duty, in consequence of his arrogating to himself the privilege of cutting up rigging, contrary to my orders, and long continued neglect of duty – August 25th.'

Certainly not all voyages to California were smooth sailing. There was a shortage of trained crews, and captains often had to put to sea with incompetent and vicious men before the mast. Captain Waterman, who had commanded the *Sea Witch* on her record passages, left New York in August 1851 in the *Challenge,* at 2,006 tons one of the largest clippers afloat. On paper he had a crew of fifty-six able seamen and eight boys, the majority of them from European countries. It was obvious their only concern was to reach the gold mines. Waterman had them mustered, and while he was telling them he expected efficiency and discipline, the chief petty officers ransacked the men's baggage in the forecastle, discovering bottles of rum, knuckle dusters and revolvers, which they dumped overboard. Only six men of this motley crew knew how to steer a ship; Captain Waterman could do no other than make them quartermasters for the voyage.

There was peace on board the *Challenge* until she was abeam of Rio de Janeiro. Then four of the crew attacked the first mate with knives, pinning him against a bulwark. Captain Waterman was taking sights on the poop when he heard cries for help. He rushed on to the main deck, grabbed an iron belaying pin and laid out the four men. Off Cape Horn three men were shaken off the yards by the plunging of the ship; one fell into the sea and was swept away by the great waves, the others were killed when their bodies hit the deck. There were no further incidents, but when the *Challenge* reached San Francisco the

The clipper *Red Jacket* built for the Australian service of Pilkington & Wilson. Here she is navigating the ice off Cape Horn; the date is August 1854.

In the later days of sail, ships such as the *Parma*, shown here, survived into the 1930s. The long, rolling swells through which she is sailing give the impression that the sea almost reaches the top of her bulwarks.

crew charged Captain Waterman with being an inhuman bully who had starved them. They gathered a mob in support; the authorities called out the militia and, with its appearance, the crew of the *Challenge* lost their liquor-induced courage and the protest petered out.

Much the same degree of disorder prevailed at the height of the Australian gold rush, and captains with unruly crews had them put in gaol on trumped-up charges of mutiny to prevent them from deserting ship in search of gold. It is timely, in shipbuilding terms also, to turn now to the Britain-to-Australia trade, as it was after the discovery of gold. In Liverpool, an enterprising young man called James Baines saw the advantages of employing big clippers in the expanding Australian passenger and cargo business, just as Duncan Dunbar before him had become disenchanted with the cumbersome East Indiaman. Baines raised enough finance to start the Black Ball Line (not to be confused with the American Black Ball Line of 1816) by ordering from Smith & Company in St John, New Brunswick, the first clipper ship to be built for the Australian trade. The *Marco Polo*, a ship of 1,622 tons, was held to be no beauty, but she immediately began to set the pace for fast passages under the British flag, reaching Melbourne in sixty-eight days and returning in seventy-four, after a voyage that had taken her round the world.

James Baines's experience with the *Marco Polo*, his judgement of the prospects for passenger and cargo traffic to Australia, and his alertness to what the competition was up to, brought him to the conclusion that the China tea clippers were too small to have profitable futures on his routes. He rightly decided that only ships of the extreme clipper type which were being built in New England would suit him. They had very fine lines, which narrowed their hulls, but they were still big ships, large enough to carry between six and seven hundred emigrants, some cargo, and the quantity of fresh water needed on a long voyage. Of all the clipper shipbuilders in the United States, three had become famous for quality of design and construction. They were William H. Webb, John W. Griffiths and Donald McKay.

It was Donald McKay who designed, built and in 1854 delivered four ships for James Baines, the *Lightning, James Baines, Donald McKay* and *Cham-*

pion of the Seas. The *Lightning* was the best of the four. When she was making ready to sail from Boston for Liverpool on 18 February 1854, a rival ship, the *Red Jacket*, owned by the Black Ball Line's strongest competitor, Pilkington and Wilson's White Star Line, was due to sail from New York the following day. The ships were evenly matched. The *Lightning* was commanded by Captain Bully Forbes; his first mate was the equally colourful Bully Bragg. The *Red Jacket* made the shorter passage to Liverpool, but the *Lightning* put up a record that for a sailing ship has stood unbroken – 436 miles for a day's run. (In the matter of speeds and distances, it is well to remember that when Nelson sailed the British fleet to the West Indies in pursuit of the French, his heavy ships-of-the-line did well to make six knots.)

The *Red Jacket* was built primarily for the Australian trade and her race with the *Lightning* was accidental. Liverpool was the birthplace of many well-known shipping companies, sail and steam. Of the personalities behind them, one of the longest lived was Sir William Forwood, who towards the end of his life put on paper memories of seventy years. In common with many pioneer shipowners his interest in ships was not confined to balance sheets. He was an enthusiastic yachtsman, and he decided to make a voyage to Australia: the *Red Jacket* appealed to him because he believed her reputation for hard sailing would give him practical knowledge of the qualities and vices of the clippers. In 1857 he joined the *Red Jacket* as a passenger bound for Australia. 'On the morning of the 20th November 1857 I embarked by a tender from the Liverpool Pierhead. It was nearly the top of high water. The crew were mustered on the forecastle, under the 1st mate. An order comes from the quarter deck. ''Heave up the anchor and get under way.'' ''Man the windlass,'' shouts the mate, and to a merry shanty:

In 1847 Paddy Murphy went to heaven
To work upon the railway,
A-working on the railway, the railway, the railway,
Oh, poor Paddy works upon the railway

the chain cable comes in with a click, click of the windlass falls. ''The anchor is aweigh, sir,'' shouts the mate. ''Heave it a-peak and cathead it,'' comes from the quarter deck, and the tug *Retriever* forges ahead and tightens the tow rope as we gather way. Bang, bang went the guns, and twice more, for we were carrying mails, and good-bye to old Liverpool.'

At this time the clipper was as near perfect as man could make her. There was still glory to come; but there were only twelve years ahead before the Suez Canal was to be opened, killing the sailing ship as the prime commercial conveyor. Before we look at the last generation of clippers, which included the *Cutty Sark,* a word must be said about the biggest wooden sailing ship ever built, Donald McKay's *Great Republic,* launched in 1853. She was 335 feet in length with a beam of 53 feet; her mainmast was 131 feet high; her tonnage was 4,555. And she had a steam-driven engine on deck to hoist the yeards and work the pumps. Donald McKay expected the *Great Republic* to become his masterpiece of ship design. It was the disappointment of his life when she caught fire and burnt out when almost ready for sea. She was salvaged and re-rigged, but on nothing like the scale of her original plan.

In the early 1860s British tea clippers introduced a new constructional feature, the composite hull, adding iron frames to a wooden ship. The China clippers combined speed, strength and carrying capacity. They were ships with shapely hulls and beautifully balanced rigs. Of the many, five stand out not only as the most graceful but as ships whose histories were interlinked. They were the *Serica* (1863), *Taeping* (1863), *Ariel* (1865), *Thermopylae* (1868) and *Cutty Sark* (1869).

The first three ships were contestants in a celebrated race from Foochow, in south-east China, to London in 1866. Clippers were, incidentally, very sensitive to the way they were trimmed, that is, how carefully the cargo was loaded so that the ship was not too much 'by the head' or too much 'by the stern'. It was common practice to balance a ship by moving varying lengths of chain cable from the chain locker in the forecastle to the stern. All three captains and their first mates watched the stowage of the tea chests with such vigilance that they might well have had spirit levels before their eyes. There is a contemporary story that Captain Keay of the *Ariel* had his cabin, which was right aft, filled with tea chests to give the ship an extra inch or two by the stern, while he moved his quarters to a passenger cabin.

The race was well documented. All her cargo stowed, hatches battened down, the *Ariel* was towed to the mouth of the Min River at 5 pm on 28 May 1866 and anchored for the night. The three ships were clear of the river mouth on 30 May and got under way within half an hour of each other. Their course lay through the islands of the South China Sea, past Anjer Point at the tip of Java, across the Indian Ocean to the Cape of Good Hope and then a straight run north of 6,000 miles. The ships seldom saw each other; they hailed other passing ships for news. Fickleness of wind and sea caused them to change positions from day to day, but all three ships hoisted signal flags at the Azores on 29 August as they passed Flores, ninety-one days out.

The *Ariel* and *Taeping* sighted the Bishop Rock Lighthouse within hours of each other on 5 September, and with the wind west-south-west they raced up the English Chanel at over thirteen knots. Nearer the French coast the *Serica* was keeping pace, but she was out of the race. This had now reached a stage that is recorded in a ship's log as 'detention'. Detenttion while taking a pilot on board at Dungeness; detention while picking up a tug off the Downs for the tow to dock; detention awaiting the dockmaster's hail to come ahead. Whether or not the *Taeping* had the better tug and the good fortune to go straight into dock, getting the edge on the *Ariel,* all that matters is that after ninety-nine days and a voyage of 16,000 miles, only twenty minutes separated the *Taeping*, the leader, from the *Ariel*.

The names of the *Cutty Sark* and *Thermopylae* have always been coupled, for they were true sister ships. Their dimensions were practically identical. In the records of their sailing there is uncanny resemblance. They had one great race, in 1872, which was also the last great race between clippers, for the Suez Canal had been open for three years and cargo steamers were rapidly securing an increasing share of all passenger and cargo traffic to India, the Far East and Australasia.

The two ships left Shanghai together. In the middle of the Indian Ocean the *Cutty Sark* lost her rudder in a gale – next to being dismasted, the worst possible mishap for a sailing ship. Captain Moodie could well have abandoned the race and crawled to a South African port. But he and his crew devised a jury rudder by cutting a spar into three pieces and lashing them together. And the *Cutty Sark* sailed on round the Cape of Good Hope. The makeshift rudder gave way when she was in the Doldrums and the repairing and refitting lost more time. But the measure of Captain Moodie's seamanship and skill as a shipmaster, and of the *Cutty Sark* as a ship, was the result of the race. The *Thermopylae* arrived in London after a voyage of 115 days. Despite her set-backs, the *Cutty Sark* was only seven days behind her.

Another clipper ship that rivalled the *Cutty Sark* in performance and popularity was the *Crusader*. She was an iron-hulled ship with a specification that exceeded 100 A-1 at Lloyds; for example, her hull plates were thicker than the rules required. The *Crusader* was built in Glasgow in 1865 for the London-to-Australia run and was bought in 1869 by the Shaw, Savill Line who transferred her to the New Zealand emigrant and cargo trade. A fast ship, on one voyage she sailed from Littleton to the Lizard in Cornwall in sixty-four days. The *Crusader* won such affection that a Clipper Ship Crusader Association was formed in 1874 by emigrants who had sailed in

her to New Zealand, an association perpetuated by later generations up to the beginning of the Second World War. The *Crusader* had a tonnage of 1,058 tons and a length of 211 feet.

One story of the interaction on shipmasters of the old and the new has been preserved in word and picture. On 14 February 1895, in foul weather, the New Zealand Shipping Company's mail steamer, the *Ruapehu*, was in the roaring forties bound for New Zealand. Her latitude was 46° 15′ south. She was carrying some auxiliary sail, which, coupled with the power of her single-screw machinery, was driving her at a steady thirteen knots.

Officers of the morning watch spotted a sailing ship astern. Their telescopes revealed her to be one of their own company's ships, the *Turakina*. Obviously she was gaining on the *Ruapehu*. The captain could hardly believe his eyes: he ordered the engine room to raise the steam pressure of the boilers to maximum; the deck crew set the topgallant sails. But the *Turakina*, in the hands of a true sail driver, Captain J.J. Hamon, continued to gain on the *Ruapehu*. Captain Hamon loosed and set the *Turakina*'s royal sails. By noon she was abreast of the *Ruapehu*; then, hauling her wind in a masterly piece of ship-handling, she surged past and crossed ahead.

It must have been a stirring sight. Later, the New Zealand Shipping Company invited the great marine artist, Frank H. Mason, to read the logs of the two ships, and from his knowledge of the southern seas to create an impression of a never-to-be-repeated event. The *Turakina*, by the way, was no newcomer to the seas. She had been built in 1868 as the *City of Perth*, and was of the same generation of clippers as the *Cutty Sark*.

In the remaining years of the nineteenth century full-rigged ships, mostly four-masted barques built first of iron, then of steel, succeeded the wooden clippers. Many had the grace of the clippers but they were strictly maids of all work, the remnants of sail now ousted by steam. They would never have survived had it not been possible to operate them

Two views of the *Herzogin Cecilie,* flagship of Gustaf Erikson's fleet; built in 1902, she went aground at Bolthead, South Devon, in 1936 and was abandoned.

economically in the Australian wool and grain trades and in the South American nitrate trade.

However, after the First World War, a man appeared who was prepared to gamble on the profitability of a fleet of sailing ships. He was a Finnish sea captain, Gustaf Erikson, who bought for a song a number of steel barques laid up in ports all over the world. Their owners were only too willing to be rid of them. Erikson's was a brave experiment: he established his fleet at Mariehamn in the Aland Islands, which lie in the Baltic between Sweden and Finland. His ships had been built in England, Scotland and, particularly, Germany, where a well-run sailing ship company, the Laeisz P-Line (so named because its ships began with the letter P) had been operating since the 1870s. Their largest ships, built towards the end of the nineteenth century, were mostly steel four-masted barques. The best-known were the *Passat, Potosi* and the *Pommern*; while another, the *Preussen,* was the only five-masted full-rigged ship ever built (although there were barque-rigged ships with five masts). The *Preussen* was wrecked in 1910; the other ships were bought by Erikson, at knock-down prices. Among them was the *Pamir,* which in 1946 began a new life as a sail-training ship; for ten years she was a floating college for hundreds of young Germans until she was overtaken by a hurricane in 1956 and sank in the North Atlantic.

Laeisz's P-line built their last sailing ship in 1926 – the *Padua,* of 3,064 tons. Five years earlier the Danish East Asiatic Company had ordered from Ramage and Ferguson in Leith a five-masted steel square-rigged ship, which they named *Kobenhavn.* These two ships were the last of their race. The *Kobenhavn* was designed primarily as a training ship. She had a short life and a disastrous end. Sixty cadets and fifteen of a permanent crew were on board when she sailed from the River Plate in South America on 14 December 1928, her destination Melbourne, where she was to load a cargo of grain for Europe. The *Kobenhavn's* last reported position was 900 miles short of the island of Tristan da Cunha. No trace was ever found.

Captain Erikson's flagship was the *Herzogin Cecilie*, built in 1902. She also had been designed as a sail training ship for the North German Lloyd Line, one of Europe's most famous companies in the North Atlantic passenger trade. The *Herzogin Cecilie* had no labour-saving devices such as mechanical deck winches to raise sail. Her original 'working' crew of sixty-five cadets was meant to earn its keep, and creature comforts were minimal. Besides the captain and four watch-keeping officers, a surgeon, purser, boatswain, and a dozen paid hands, the *Herzogin Cecilie* carried two officer instructors. But when Erikson bought her, such lavish manning was out of the question. She went to sea with a crew of twenty-five; there was no feather-bedding for men who sailed with Erikson.

Two other Erikson ships were the *Archibald Russell*, of 1905, the last four-masted barque to be built for a British owner, J. Hardie & Company, of Glasgow. She was a product of the famous shipyard of Scotts at Greenock, founded in 1711. The other was the *Moshulu*, another Scottish-built ship, which won the last grain race from Australia in 1939.

In this story of nineteenth-century sail the main emphasis has been on square-rigged ships. The fore-and-aft rig is equally significant, however, and there are many classes, of which the most important is the schooner. A schooner is a vessel with more than one fore-and-aft mast. Schooners have had many uses — for commerce, piracy, privateering, slavery, and as pilot boats. Four-masted schooners were common in Europe, particularly Scandinavia. The schooner won most favour in the United States, and perhaps its most successful role was as a pilot boat. Pilot boats had to keep station, awaiting the arrival of ships and taking on board pilots who had brought ships out of port, in all weathers. They were fast and manoeuvrable. They had long natural lives, of between fifteen and twenty years, but by the very nature of their task, exposed to gales and other hazards, some failed to last their time. For example, on the New York pilot station between 1838 and 1860, fifteen boats were

When sail beat steam: the *Turakina* surges past the mail steamer *Ruapehu* in 1895. The painting of this extraordinary event was commissioned from the marine artist Frank H. Mason by the New Zealand Shipping Company, which owned both ships.

The *Cutty Sark,* fully restored at Greenwich, London. Her masts and spars, square-rigged, show the beauty of the late clippers.

A model of one of the most grotesque ships in the history of sail, the seven-masted schooner *Thomas W. Lawson,* built in America in 1902. She carried a crew of no more than fifteen men.

lost. Nevertheless, schooners continued in this work up to the time when powered boats replaced them. It has been said, by the way, that America's most successful contenders for the America's Cup were, in the early days of the competition, modelled on the lines of the pilot schooner.

Schooners inevitably became larger. There were massive five-masters, one six- and even one seven-master. The six-masted schooner, the *Wyoming,* was built in Bath, Maine, for New York owners in 1909. The *Wyoming* and other large American schooners were designed to carry cargo at more economical rates than the clipper, now superseded by the steamship. By sailing ship standards, the *Wyoming* was a big ship. She was 3,730 tons gross and could carry 5,000 tons of cargo, her crew complement being only twelve men. She traded for fifteen years, until she was wrecked on the American coast in 1924 on passage from Chesapeake Bay with a cargo of coal.

But the seven-master, *Thomas W. Lawson,* was a flop – or what a seaman would call a cranky ship. No captain was happy with her: she was sluggish and difficult to handle in spite of the steam winches installed to raise sail. Built of steel in 1902 at Quincy,

Massachusetts, for the Coastwise Transportation Company, she was registered at Boston. Her dimensions are worth quoting, for she was the only one of her type ever built. She was 375 feet 7 inches in length, her beam was 50 feet and her tonnage 5,218. Her life was short – she was wrecked in 1907.

In retrospect, the thirty-year period between 1845 and 1875 represents the finest phase in close on six thousand years of sailing ships. In that short space of time the clipper was supreme; it was a time of perfection in ship design and in the union of ships, men and the winds. Joseph Conrad had the sensitivity of the artist and the expertise of a master mariner. He should have the last word on sail. 'A ship is not a slave. You must make her easy in a seaway, you must never forget that you owe her the fullest share of your thought, of your skill, of your self-love. If you remember that obligation, naturally and without effort, as if it were an instinctive feeling of your inner life, she will sail, stay, run for you as long as she is able, or, like a sea-bird going to rest upon the angry waves, she will lay out the heaviest gale that ever made you doubt living long enough to see another sunrise.'

Fighting ships (1700-1906)

Nelson's flagship *Victory*, as she may be seen today, immaculately reconstructed in the dockyard at Portsmouth.

Lying dismasted during the
War of 1812, the British
frigate *Guerrière*, soundly
defeated, surrenders to the
American frigate *Constitution*.

During the eighteenth century the 'battleship' of the day, the ship-of-the-line, showed little change in hull design. There were refinements in rigging, in the set of the sails and in the mechanics of steering. The design of guns, cannon and shot were also virtually static. The only significant progress was the invention in mid-century of the carronade, which hurled a cannon ball at low velocity and had great powers of destruction at short range.

In an earlier chapter it was said that the *Sovereign of the Seas* of 1637, a ship of 1,683 tons (and 100 guns) was so in advance of her time that she could have fought at Trafalgar in 1805. Indeed by comparison, the largest ship in the Royal Navy in 1700 was little

heavier, at 1,809 tons, and also had 100 guns; at the end of the century the size of the largest ship had increased only to 2,600 tons, and the number of guns to 120.

The fact was that the sailing fighting ship was approaching the limit of its capabilities. When the mechanically propelled ship came to the seas, and grew in size and speed with the advance of technology, she acquired an ever-increasing mobility. Neither the sailing ship nor even the most persuasive master could command the winds to blow more strongly, or be certain that they would blow in a desired direction. It was not uncommon for sailing ships to be denied entry to the English Channel, for example, by

The *Agincourt*, from a portrait
dated 1868. At over 400 feet
she and her sister ships
Minotaur and *Northumberland*
were the longest single-screw
warships ever built.

a sudden shift of wind from west to east. Joseph
Conrad had a very poor opinion of the character of
the East Wind: 'I have seen him, like a wizened rob-
ber sheik of the sea, hold up large caravans of ships
to the number of three hundred or more at the very
gates of the English Channel. Every day added to our
numbers. In knots and groups and straggling parties
we flung to and fro before the closed gate. And meantime the outward-bound ships passed, running
through our humiliated ranks under all the canvas
they could show.'

If there was inertia in basic design, this was not
true of decorating and carving. The prestige ship
retained a stubborn appeal. Immense sums were

spent on elaborate carvings and decoration, particularly on the stern galleries, which in big ships extended to four tiers. All sense of the warlike purpose
of these ships escaped the heady enthusiasm of some
of their artists, and reached absurdity when the
Admiral's state cabin in the *Royal Sovereign* of 1701
was decorated with painted murals.

About the middle of the eighteenth century we
find increasing mention of frigates, although ideas
varied at the time about the size, shape, rig and gun-
power. The 'fighting' frigate was in fact a ship with
two decks: on one she carried her main armament,
which ranged between twenty and fifty guns. France
developed the frigate with great success and British

Chivalry in war: a painting by G. Webster of the famous action between the *Shannon* and the *Chesapeake*. It bears the inscription 'To Captain Broke, the Officers, Seamen and Marines of His Majesty's Ship Shannon. This View of their Boarding and Capturing the American United States Frigate The Chesapeake, off Boston on the 1st June 1813 after a sanguinary Conflict of only fifteen minutes is with respect Dedicated to them, and the Admirers of British Valor by their obedient Servant' (signed G. Webster).

designs were based on the French forty-gun *Embuscade*, captured in 1746. In the Royal Navy frigates were adopted with caution but, in 1757, the *Southampton*, first of a new class, performed admirably. The value of frigates was proved in the American War of Independence, when as many as sixty, developed from the *Southampton*'s original design, were in service. A well-handled frigate could turn and manoeuvre with the slickness of a yacht, and outsail and capture any merchant ship.

Fine frigates were built in America towards the end of the century. They were the right ships for a new navy because of their flexibility in most conditions of wind and sea. They caused havoc among the French privateers and were invaluable during the war of 1812, when they harassed British shipping. There were duels between individual ships. In July 1812 the British frigate *Guerrière* (a ship captured from the French) found herself faced by the formidable American frigate *Constitution*, newly commissioned. The *Guerrière* fought gamely until she was dismasted and sunk. Then there were the exploits of the *Chesapeake*, built in 1799. She began in the Caribbean with assaults on pirates; moved to the Mediterranean as the flagship of the American Commodore Richard Morris, blockading Tripoli in 1802. In 1812 she pursued and captured five British merchant ships.

Possibly the greatest single action between sailing ships, fought honourably and to the rules, was the encounter of the *Chesapeake* and the British frigate *Shannon*, under the command of Captain Broke, who was patrolling the seas off Boston. He issued a challenge to Captain Lawrence of the *Chesapeake*; and on 1 June 1813 the two ships met fifteen miles off Boston to fight an engagement that was evenly matched, for the ships carried fifty guns apiece. The action was fast and furious: in less than fifteen minutes the *Shannon* had overcome the *Chesapeake*. Both captains were severely injured and Captain Lawrence died of his wounds. When he was struck down, Captain Lawrence uttered a phrase that became famous in America: 'Don't give up the ship'.

By that point in history Trafalgar had been fought and won; the last shots had been fired at Waterloo. About six hundred and fifty British warships of all types were in commission. They could not be 'mothballed' – as British and American ships were after the Second World War. There was nothing for it but to break them up, keep the most modern in reserve with maintenance crews and retain a token force of some twenty ships-of-the-line to patrol the seas and keep the peace.

For centuries, the sailing fighting ship had been the only fighting ship. Tradition dies hard and resistance is human and instinctive to any kind of major change, particularly in highly disciplined forces accustomed to inflexible authority. It is not to be wondered that the years after Waterloo were years of indecision. The cause was the emergence of the steamship. The period 1815 – 35 was one of unsettlement for many directors of naval construction. The more enlightened faced powerful opposition to the idea of steam; they were aware that it had a future in ship propulsion but were equally aware that wooden paddle-wheelers could never become ships-of-the-line. They were fit only as auxiliaries, for their paddle-boxes were not only frail and vulnerable but they drastically reduced the number of guns by dividing the ship amidships.

Compromise exposes weaknesses. The first half of

The British ship-of-the-line *Victoria* (1859), the last wooden three-decker with auxiliary power to join the Royal Navy.

The French frigate *La Gloire*, built in 1859; she was the first ironclad to be completed.

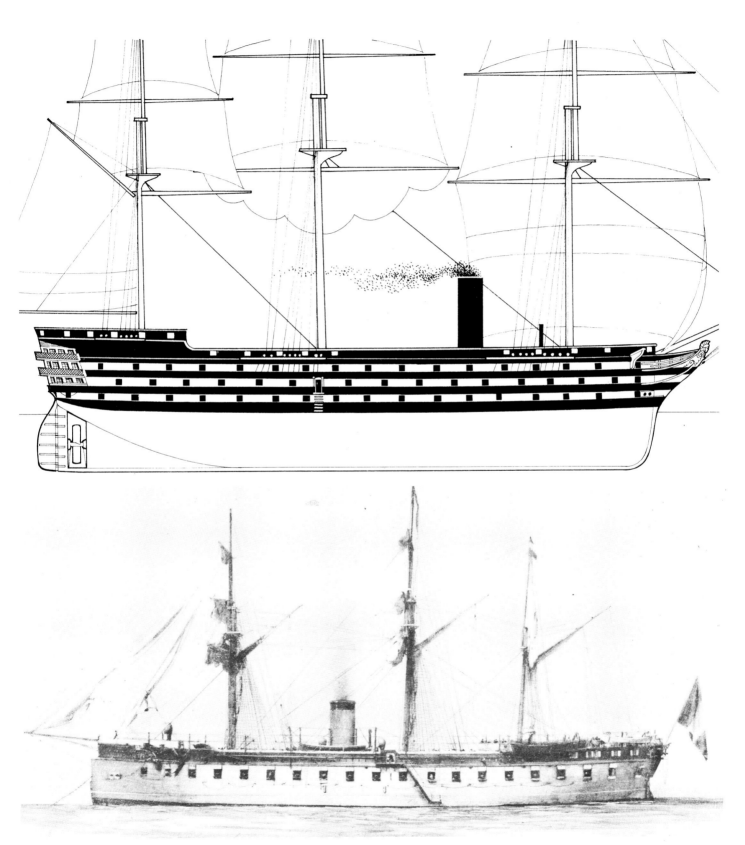

Nelson's deployment of the British fleet at Trafalgar, in two lines ahead: this formation divided the combined French and Spanish fleets. Nelson led the port, Collingwood the starboard van. An important ship appears in the group of four to the left of the picture: she is the *Euryalus*, whose commander, Captain Blackwood, had signalled to Nelson the precise arrangement of the enemy fleet as it left Cadiz harbour. *Inset:* Nelson's Flagship *Victory* at the battle of Trafalgar.

ENEMY'S VAN

Santissima Trinidada, 130.

Bucentaure, &c. Adm. Villeneuve.

Sirius, 36.

Naiad, 38.

Euryalus, 36.

Phœbe, 36.

Entreprenante Cutter.

Africa, 64.

Pickle Schooner.

1 *Victory, &c. Lord Nelson.*

2 *Temeraire, 98.*

3 *Neptune, 98.*

4 *Conqueror, 74.*

5 *Leviathan, 74.*

6 *Ajax, 74.*

7 *Orion, 74.*

8 *Agamemnon, 64.*

9 *Minotaur, 74.*

10 *Spartiate, 74.*

11 *Britannia, 100.*

Pineapple, Achates, 10.
Agamemnon, 112.

Santa Anna, 112.

ENEMY'S REAR

Royal Sovereign, 100.
L'Adm.l Collingwood

L'Achille, 74.
blown up during the Action.

Mars, 74.

Belle isle, 74.

Tonnant, 80.

Bellerophon, 74.

Colossus, 74.

Achille, 74.

Polyphemus, 64.

Revenge, 74.

Swiftsure, 74.

Defence, 74.

Thunderer, 74.

Defiance, 74.

Prince, 98.

Dreadnought, 98.

1

2

3

the nineteenth century produced an uncoordinated succession of fighting ships that were a hotchpotch of wooden sailing ships converted to propeller-driven steamships; of wooden ships-of-the-line retaining sail; iron frigates, and even a steam-assisted ship-of-the-line built after the Crimean War (1853 – 6). If this assortment is bewildering to our eyes how much more difficult must it have been for naval constructors and for the captains and crews who handled these hybrid ships. With hindsight it is possible to say that too much was happening at once in those days of the first Industrial Revolution.

In the field of armament, the French had been experimenting with explosive shells in the early 1700s. By the late 1820s the French armament developer, Paixhans, had devised an explosive shell and an incendiary to go with it. They were tested exhaustively and proved without doubt that no wooden warship, either sail-driven or with auxiliary steam engines, would survive their fire. Iron frigates were equally vulnerable, for their iron hulls were wafer-thin and without armoured protection of any kind. Many were converted to troopships, including the luckless *Birkenhead*, which ran aground in South Africa in 1852. Vast amounts of money were spent in putting propeller-driven machinery into wooden warships of all types. The last wooden, screw-driven frigate was the *Newcastle*, completed in 1874.

Meanwhile the steam-driven merchant ship had developed rapidly. Regular sailings, iron hulls, propellers and reliable machinery were defeating the valiant performances of the clippers. A post-mortem on the Crimean War opened the eyes of many people. Merchant steamships were there in large numbers as troopships; the Cunarder *Andes* was employed in carrying reinforcements into the Black Sea, towing sailing ships, and bringing batches of wounded and cholera victims to Scutari.

Steam, iron and then steel were advancing inexorably. In France another hybrid was built, but with a difference. The frigate *La Gloire* had a wooden hull, but she had the protection of four and a half

The British nuclear-powered submarine *Revenge* at her commissioning ceremony in 1969, completing a building programme of four similar submarines, the others being *Resolution, Repulse,* and *Renown.* They each carry sixteen Polaris missiles, and have six torpedo tubes.

inches of armoured plate. *La Gloire* carried sufficient coal to stay at sea for a month at a speed of eight knots. Under full power she could reach thirteen knots. That same year, 1859, the Royal Navy had commissioned the *Victoria,* the last wooden three-decked ship with auxiliary power. Britain's reply to *La Gloire,* also laid down in 1859, was the *Warrior,* the first of the Royal Navy's ironclads. Wood was at last discarded for the hulls of front-line warships. Now sail became the auxiliary, and the *Warrior,* for one, relied on her machinery. This was of 5,270 horsepower and gave her a speed of fourteen knots. Her guns, though, were fixed weapons, and the *Warrior* herself had to be aimed at the enemy to bring the guns to bear.

It was left to America to focus attention on the principle of mounting heavy guns in an armoured revolving turret. In a bizarre engagement during the American Civil War between two strange armoured craft built of iron, the Federal *Monitor* demonstrated

the tactical mobility of her revolving turret compared with the fixed armament of the Confederate ship *Merrimac.* The action was indecisive but John Ericsson, the Swedish-American inventor, had proved the effectiveness of his turret design.

From time to time in these pages the closeness in appearance of sail-driven warships and sail-driven merchant ships has been commented upon. Now, in 1873, the ship-of-the-line became the battleship or ironclad, which in the new navy spawned all manner of offensive craft, destroyers, cruisers, battle cruisers, submarines and, eventually, aircraft carriers. The merchant ship went her own way and diversified, producing ships designed for specific commercial purposes, from bulk carriers to cable layers.

There is no mistaking the function of the British ironclad *Devastation,* of 1873; an arresting feature was the absence of masts. The Admiralty had at last shed auxiliary sail. In that bold step they accepted the power and reliability of steam, preceding by some

years the abandonment of sails by merchant ships (passengers liked the reassurance of a spread of canvas).

The *Devastation's* appearance, construction and statistics are interesting because she broke with the past and became a model for the future. She was 285 feet long and 62.3 feet wide – proportions of nearly four to one that gave her great stability as a gun platform for her four twelve-inch guns; these were mounted in twin turrets protected by iron armoured plate between ten and fourteen inches thick. The armour on her hull was between eight and a half and twelve inches thick.

After the *Devastation* there began the nineteenth-century naval equivalent of the twentieth-century space race. One country had only to build a ship of the character of the *Devastation* and a bigger and more powerful ship would appear. The Italians in 1876 produced the *Duilio* and the *Dandalo*, which combined high speed and heavy guns. For their time, they had the mammoth armament of four fifteen-inch

guns in twin turrets, and could reach fifteen knots. In 1891 the Americans launched their *Indiana* class of ironclad, mounting four thirteen-inch guns; the French in 1893 produced the *Charles-Martel* class with two twelve-inch and two eleven-inch guns.

Progress in the quality of steel, the invention of the steam turbine by Sir Charles Parsons, improvement in the rifling of guns and in the penetrative power of shells and torpedoes made an anachronism of the term 'ironclad'. In 1906 Britain revolutionized the heavy fighting ship; the ironclad became the dreadnought. And it was a ship of this name, *Dreadnought,* that ushered in the age of the fast, heavily armed and protected ship-of-the-line – the capital ship or battleship. The *Dreadnought's* steam turbines of 23,000 horsepower drove her at twenty-one knots. She had ten twelve-inch guns in five turrets and five underwater torpedo tubes.

To carry forward the story of the fighting ship in all its forms from the eventful date of 1906 would fill a book in itself. But briefly, let us conclude this

Dreadnought (1906), the
British battleship that
introduced to the world's
navies the fast, heavily
armoured capital ship. She
was a product of the genius of
Admiral Lord Fisher.

chapter with a word about nuclear-powered fighting ships.

To see more clearly the evolution of the later vessel, the British nuclear submarine *Revenge* of 1969 is here set alongside her predecessor, the battleship *Revenge* of 1894. The advances in the technologies of propelling machinery and fire power are illuminating:

Revenge 1894

Length	380 feet
Displacement	14,150 tons
Machinery	Triple-expansion reciprocating engines
Fuel	Coal
Speed	18 knots
Cost	£839,000
Armament	The battleship's 4 13½-inch guns fired a broadside of just over 2 tons

Revenge 1969

Length	425 feet
Displacement	7,500 tons (on the surface)
Machinery	Nuclear power
Fuel	Atomic energy
Speed	Over 20 knots submerged
Cost	£15,000,000
Armament	The submarine's nuclear missiles can deliver the equivalent of 700,000 tons of high explosives, greater than all the explosives fired by all sides in the two world wars

Finally, let us take a look at the United States' great aircraft carrier *Enterprise*. She displaces 83,350 tons; is 1,102 feet long; her eight nuclear reactors drive four propellers for a speed of thirty-five knots. Her power plant develops 300,000 horsepower. And her consort, the *Admiral Nimitz*, will be able to continue voyaging for thirteen years without the need to refuel. If we assume that a ship's life span is twenty-five years, the *Admiral Nimitz* will require only one refuelling operation in her entire career.

The 83,350-ton American
nuclear-powered aircraft
carrier *Enterprise*, her
enormous flight deck arrayed
with aircraft. Members of her
crew of 4,600 form the US
flag to record a span of
American history from 1776
to 1963.

The modern commercial ship

The *Great Britain* in 1970: at sea once more, she is towed back from the Falkland Islands to the drydock at Bristol in which she was built.

1. Robert Fulton's *Clermont* (1807): this engraving features in detail the feathering of the paddle wheels and the single-cylinder engine that first drove the ship; later twin-cylinder compound engines were installed.

2. The *Charlotte Dundas* (1801), a Clyde canal tug acknowledged to have been the first practical steamboat.

3. The paddle-steamer *Enterprise:* she sailed from England to Calcutta via the Cape of Good Hope in 113 days, a brave if not record-breaking performance which won her owners a handsome consolation prize from sponsors in Bengal, who originally offered 20,000 rupees for the first passage taking not more than seventy days.

Experiments with steam engines to drive boats were made simultaneously in Britain and America towards the end of the eighteenth century. In Scotland William Symington produced in 1801 the *Charlotte Dundas*, a Clyde canal tug described in the current *Encyclopaedia Britannica* as 'the first practical steamboat'. Earlier, in America in 1788, John Fitch had built the steamboat *Experiment* to ply between Philadelphia and Trenton, but she was not a commerical success.

These were the practical beginnings of mechanically propelled ships. The first commercially successful river paddle-steamers were built within five years of each other in America and Britain. Robert Fulton's *Clermont* (or *North River*) appeared in 1807 on the Hudson River, and Henry Bell's *Comet* in 1812 on the Clyde in Scotland.

They were prophetic ventures. Once the marine steam engine and boiler had developed sufficient horsepower and endurance to be trusted to the oceans, the North Atlantic was the natural route. It has become a cliché to describe the Atlantic ferry as producing a great trading link between the peoples of the old world and the new; and as the route that brought life to America. But this need not diminish the truth of the statement. The emigration movement to the United States assumed significant proportions in the late 1840s and 1850s. Its impetus, checked by the American Civil War, was resumed in 1865. The movement reached its peak in 1906; before that, in the sixty years from 1840 to 1900, the population of the United States increased from 17,069,453 to 75,994,575. It was a period when some 20,000,000 immigrants entered the country.

In the 1820s the American Baltimore sailing packets were drawing traffic from the British 'coffin brigs' – unseaworthy ships that carried His Majesty's Mails – and the paddle-steamer was struggling to find its sea-legs. An attempt to 'steam' across the Atlantic in 1819 by the Dutch-owned *Savannah* proved uneconomic. She was rigged as a three-masted sailing ship and her paddles, which were detachable, were

1. Henry Bell's *Comet*, Britain's first commercially successful river paddle-steamer, built for the Clyde in 1812.

2. A contemporary print of the *Sirius*, owned by the St George's Steam Packet Company: designed for no more than the cross-channel service to Dublin, she became one of the Atlantic pioneers by sailing from Cork to New York in 1838; she was laden with so much coal (450 tons) that she very nearly foundered.

3. River and deep-sea ships designed by the American pioneer Robert Fulton (1765–1815), who introduced the first American riverboat, the *Clermont*, and also brought steam to the Mississippi River.

merely an aid. They were used only on three and a half of the twenty-nine days of her crossing from Savannah to Liverpool. She nevertheless proved a novelty to the men of the semaphore station at Cape Clear, Ireland, who, when they saw the *Savannah* approaching, belching clouds of smoke, thought she was on fire and sent a cutter to the rescue. But the *Savannah*'s effort was important because it caused men of imagination to take notice. Even in the early days, when the steamship suffered abuse and mockery – being called anything from 'steam kettle' to 'diabolical creation of Lucifer' – men of foresight grasped that steam could be applied to ships to bring commercial success. These men included Robert Napier, Samuel Cunard, Isambard Kingdom Brunel, John Scott Russell and William Froude.

Robert Napier built the engines and advised on the size of ship required to run a weekly Atlantic service from Liverpool to Halifax and Boston with four identical ships. This project was the brainchild of Samuel Cunard, whose *Britannia* began the first regular Atlantic sailings with steamships, and the first action in the battle for supremacy between sail and steam

1

2

3

1. The *Stockholmshaxan* (Witch of Stockholm), a converted sloop. Produced by Samuel Owen in 1816 she was driven by a primitive engine·but used a propeller rather than a paddle; the propeller had four wooden blades and was fitted into a frame of cast iron.

2. The *Great Eastern* was among the most photographed of all ships. She has also an entire art gallery to herself. None of these impressions disguises her ugliness. This hull and rigging plan is the that the *Great Eastern* was an iron box with no shapely curve to delight ship lovers. Her funnels resemble Victorian factory chimneys. But the detail repays study: the hull is 680 feet long; one of the enormous paddle boxes, 58 feet in diameter; the propeller itself, 24 feet in diameter; and the sail plan, by W.S. Lindsay's calculations as much as 65,000 square feet, combine to reveal the scale of Brunel and Scott Russell's concept.

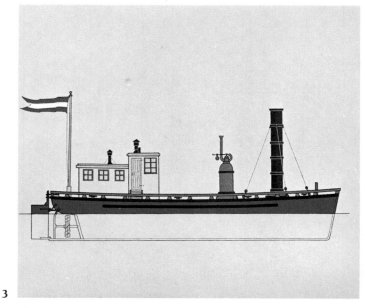

1

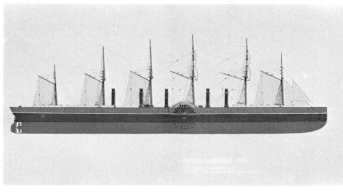

2

3

3. The *Robert F. Stockton*, built in England in 1838 for the USA, crossed the Atlantic under sail in 1839 and took up service towing canal barges. Her claim to distinction is that she was the first iron-hulled ship to cross the Atlantic and the first merchant ship to be driven by a screw propeller.

4. The *Thomas Anderson* (1889), a steel ship built in Sunderland; she had a single propeller, driven by a three-cylinder expansion engine, and she retained auxiliary sail.

4

A poster of the early 1860s; before the days of advertising agencies, steamship companies were obliged to use their own imaginations in selling the superior accommodation and 'full dietary' that they offered. The *Sidon* was built in 1861 for the Cunard Line. This poster, even with its imperfect spelling, gives an indication of the inroads that the steamship was achieving in the 1860s against the last of the sailing clippers.

Portrait of the great engineer Isambard Kingdom Brunel (1806–59).

on the Atlantic. Brunel, inventor, builder of bridges and steamships, and Scott Russell, scientist, engineer and student of the structure of ships, dedicated themselves to improving the strength and seaworthiness of the steam-powered vessel. They pressed the case for iron hulls and propellers against wooden hulls and paddle-wheels. William Froude was a pioneer of the test tank, in which models of ships were drawn back and forth to establish the fitness of their hull-form and the horsepower that would be needed to drive them. Froude fought the old rule-of-thumb conservatism to win recognition for the value of a pre-tested model. Today, of course, no one would dream of building a ship without examining the prior performance of a wax or wooden model moved by a gantry over a water-filled test tank, the latter being equipped to simulate all conditions of sea from flat calm to hurricane.

Elsewhere, inventors and innovators were busy. The first steamship to be built of iron, the *Aaron Manby* (1822), was fashioned in sections in Staffordshire and put together in the Surrey Commercial Docks on the Thames. She thus became the first prefabricated ship; on completion she was delivered to French owners, who employed her on the Seine between Paris and Le Havre. More ambitious aims were aroused in 1823 when a group of rich men in Bengal offered a prize of 20,000 rupees to the first steamship to open a service from England to Calcutta; the passage not to exceed seventy days. A Royal Navy lieutenant, James Johnston, with a group of associates, took up the offer and a 404-ton paddle-wheeler named the *Enterprise* made the voyage from Falmouth to Calcutta via the Cape of Good Hope, a distance of 13,700 miles, in 113 days – not a record-breaking performance but a brave effort that won her half the prize. The *Enterprise* was not efficient enough to make a profit, however, and she was sold to the Bengal government for $40,000.

There are many examples of pioneer ships such as the *Enterprise*, but in this short review of the progress of steam and motor-driven merchant ships it is

The *Aaron Manby* (1822), the first iron-built ship. She was also the first prefabricated ship; put together on the Thames she took up a service between Paris and Le Havre.

Brunel's *Great Britain* (1845): she was an iron ship, screw-propelled, and was built for the Atlantic. In the beginning she had six masts, then later she was driven aground at Dundrum Bay in Ireland, salvaged and re-rigged. She finished her working life in the Falkland Islands in 1886.

95

The Pacific Mail Steam-Ship Company's *Great Republic*, built in 1886 to fulfil the company's commitment to run a trans-Pacific mail service. She and her sister ships came under criticism because they were wooden-hulled ships, driven by the then outdated 'walking-beam' engine.

The American *Savannah* arriving in Liverpool in 1819 after what was technically the first Atlantic crossing by a steamship; the *Savannah*, however, only used her machinery on three and a half days out of twenty-four.

necessary to choose key ships and dates. The *Sirius* and *Great Western* – the latter one of Brunel's designs – both made an Atlantic voyage in 1838, using steam there and back. Brunel's triumph was the *Great Britain* of 1845; she was built of iron, propeller-driven and easily the largest ship of her time. Brunel had the confidence to trust to iron and the screw propeller when the majority of shipowners were committed to wooden hulls and paddle-wheels. It is certain that the *Great Britain* would have continued in Atlantic service had she not been driven aground in 1846 on the Irish coast at Dundrum Bay. She was refloated the following year, but her owners were in equally low water and the Great Western Company disposed of her for service in the Australian trade. She had been built with six masts; she was re-rigged with three masts, then converted into a sailing ship – and ended her days, or so it seemed at the time, in 1886 as a coal hulk in the Falkland Islands. But in 1970, her tough iron hull intact, the *Great Britain* was towed back to Britain, and now lies in Bristol in the drydock in which she was built.

If creature comforts for sailing ship passengers in the 1840s were meagre even in the first class, travellers in steamers fared little better. Dickens' opinions of the *Britannia* in his *American Notes* are well known. Another author, Lyons MacLeod, wrote of his passage in the steamship *Ireland*, owned by Lindsay's Mail Line. He sailed from Dartmouth in 1856 for Cape Town, occupying 'a miserable doghole' six feet long and five feet wide, so uncomfortable that he found it less trying if he put his mattress on the deck. There were no lights in MacLeod's section of the ship because the candles were too big for the candlesticks in the cabins. His steward 'fertile in imagination produced as a substitute for candlesticks a quantity of tin spittoons which had been sent on board by mistake'. In early steamships trading to South America, the decks were sweetened and fumigated by swinging stoves. Rats were troublesome; they ate the mail bags, gnawed the corks of champagne bottles and raided the pantries. A regulation followed – captains were instructed to see that they had one or more cats on board before sailing from Southampton.

In the 1850s most passengers were at least spared the discomforts of changing ships and crossing an isthmus that faced travellers to India and the Far East who chose the Mediterranean route. The 250-mile run from Alexandria to Suez, via Cairo, required over three days of travel, allowing for rest periods.

There was at that time a growing market for high-value cargo, and shippers were prepared to pay higher freight charges for delivery speedier than by the Cape route. In the 1850s there was no railway link across the isthmus of Suez. Before the opening of the Suez Canal, up to 3,000 camels carried cargo from Alexandria to a single ship waiting at Suez. Even coal went that way, for sailing ships could not beat against the trade winds blowing towards India across the Indian Ocean, nor make their way up the Red Sea.

In another part of the world there was another isthmus – at Panama. The strip of land between the Caribbean and the Pacific was not as wide as the isthmus of Suez, but the terrain was mountainous, thickly forested, and mosquito-ridden. Mules and canoes alone made the journey until a semblance of a road was constructed. When the Californian goldrush was in its stride, a three-way route pattern, competing with the clipper trade, became profitable. Thousands of prospectors from the southern United States used Royal Mail Line ships to take them to Chagres, on the isthmus; they then sailed on to San Francisco from Panama with the American Pacific Mail Steam-Ship Company. The third tie-up was from the west coast of South America, where the Pacific Steam Navigation Company, operating under Royal Charter, brought traffic north to Panama, some to cross the isthmus and sail for England, some to join the throngs bound for the gold mines.

In 1853, the Peninsular & Oriental Steam Navigation Company built for their Mediterranean route to India a splendid ship named *Himalaya*, of 3,438 tons; then the largest ship in the world, she had been expensive to build (she cost £132,000) and she proved

The *Great Eastern*, a giant of a ship built by Brunel in 1858, was so far ahead of her time in sheer size that her statistics must appear meaningless unless they are related to the general growth of the steamship, as the diagram indicates, beginning with Brunel's own successful *Great Western* of 1838. In 1854, sixteen years after the *Great Western*, the P & O Company built the *Himalaya*, a ship almost twice the length and two and a half times the tonnage of the *Great Western*. The *Himalaya* was the largest ship in the world. Four years later the *Great Eastern* was launched. She was twice the length of the *Himalaya* and, by the measurement of the day, more than six times her tonnage. Forty years passed before her length was exceeded – by the White Star liner *Oceanic* in 1899. And it was not until 1907 that her tonnage was surpassed; that record fell to the Cunarder *Lusitania*.

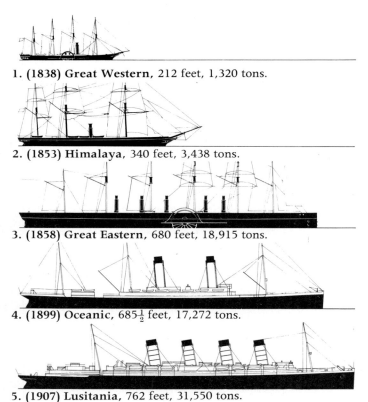

1. (1838) **Great Western**, 212 feet, 1,320 tons.

2. (1853) **Himalaya**, 340 feet, 3,438 tons.

3. (1858) **Great Eastern**, 680 feet, 18,915 tons.

4. (1899) **Oceanic**, 685½ feet, 17,272 tons.

5. (1907) **Lusitania**, 762 feet, 31,550 tons.

expensive to operate. She was an iron, propeller-driven ship, carried 200 first-class passengers, 1,000 tons of cargo and 1,200 tons of coal for fuel. With this load she could maintain fourteen knots; and the addition of a full spread of sail raised her speed to sixteen and a half knots, quite an achievement for a steamship of the early 1850s. In common with dozens of other merchant ships, the British government requisitioned her as a troopship in the Crimean War; the P & O were happy to release her and struck a bargain when they sold her to the government for almost as much as she cost to build. To the Admiralty she was further proof of the value of iron propeller ships. She was also notable in another way. Placed alongside the first ironclad, HMS *Warrior* of 1860, the hull and rig of the *Himalaya* are similar. This was in fact the last occasion in the history of the fighting ship and the merchant ship when one could reasonably be taken for the other.

The steam-powered merchant ship was plodding ahead; some time was to elapse before she caught up with the clippers, but the outcome was not in doubt. The repeal, in Britain, of the Navigation Acts, and gold discoveries made in the United States and Australia provided injections of hope for the clippers, just as the Crimean War opened the Admiralty's eyes to the distinctive contribution and support that merchant ships could give to men-of-war.

The American Pacific Mail Steam-Ship Company had been active since 1847, and their *California* was the first steamship to appear on the Pacific, in 1848. Because of the distance between Panama and San Francisco repair and coaling depots had to be set up in these ports. There was also a base at Astoria, in Oregon, to service a feeder line from San Francisco. These establishments were essential in the early years of the company in the 1850s. They were expensive years, too, for the coal for the ships had to be routed round Cape Horn.

After the Civil War the United States government invited tenders for a mail service between San Francisco and Hong Kong, with a call at Yokohama. In 1886 – 7 the Pacific Mail company's tender was accepted and four wooden paddle-driven ships were constructed, the largest wooden merchant ships ever built. The company came under fire for building wooden paddle-ships, but up to that time technical development in the use of iron hulls and screw propellers had not been as rapid in the United States as in Europe. Moreover, the *Great Republic* and her sister ships were driven by 'walking-beam' engines, which were economical to operate. There was no hankering after a Pacific version of the Blue Riband of the Atlantic. The distances were so much greater that a coal-fired ship stocked with fuel for a voyage of 5,000 miles, compared with the 3,000 miles of the Atlantic would have had little revenue-earning cargo space if powerful – and bulky – coal-consuming machinery had been installed.

The American author, Richard Henry Dana, travelled to Europe in 1856 when the battle between sail and steam was at its height. His biographer, C.F.

Adams, quotes his description of arriving at Liverpool: 'we notice with pride that nearly half the ships have the Yankee flag, and those generally the smartest looking vessels'. Twenty-five years later the scene was very different. Steam had won the battle, and European flags were dominant on the Atlantic. Nonetheless, in the USA one man in particular stands out as a continuing believer in the revival of American interest in Atlantic steamships, an interest diminished by the failure of the Collins Line in 1858. He was Clement A. Griscom, who was one of the driving forces behind the start of the American Line in 1871. He was then only thirty years of age; at twenty-two he had become a partner in a firm of shipping merchants, Peter Wright & Sons.

On the Atlantic, there was the continuing pursuit of the Blue Riband for the fastest passage to and from Europe and the United States. Fractions of a day separated the performances of the ships, then driven by reciprocating engines, with triple and quadruple expansion cylinders whose giant, glistening steel connecting-rods were a delight to watch as they swept up and down to turn the propeller shaft. A celebrated ship of the 1890s was the North German Lloyd Line's *Kaiser Wilhelm der Grosse*, which covered the 3,065 miles from Sandy Hook Light to the Needles in five days seventeen hours eight minutes at an average speed of 22.35 knots. Atlantic 'racing' was a serious business; minutes counted.

The North Atlantic route aroused national rivalry; this was true also of the Britain-to-South Africa trade. In 1857, the Union Line won the mail contract to South Africa and outpaced its rivals until Donald Currie, a man experienced in commercial shipping after twenty years with the Cunard Line, began operations to South Africa in 1872. He eventually formed the Castle Line which challenged the Union Line for nearly thirty years until the two companies merged as the Union-Castle Line in 1900. During that period, the discovery of diamonds and gold in South Africa expanded the demand for steamship services, just as gold discoveries in the USA and Australia in mid-century had stimulated a similar flood of emigrant traffic.

Then, with the twentieth century in its infancy, a new method of propulsion appeared that overnight changed naval architects' and marine engineers' concepts of power and speed. This was the steam turbine, invented by Sir Charles Parsons. Time and time again he had tried to interest designers, shipbuilders, and the Admiralty in his turbine, which worked on the principle of steam under pressure being forced through a series of movable and fixed blades; in effect the steam 'bounced' off the fixed blades and turned the shaft to which the movable blades were attached. The steam passed through three stages of pressure – high, medium and low – and every pound of steam pressure was made to work. The result – more compact machinery and higher speeds. Parsons had built a prototype craft 100 feet long, which he named *Turbinia*, and, in 1897, boldly choosing time and place, he opened up her engines to maximum power and swept between the lines of British warships anchored off Spithead for review by Queen Victoria. The *Turbinia* reached 34.5 knots; not a single ship was fast enough to give chase. The outcome was an immediate demand for Parsons' turbine. Enough to say that the Cunard liner *Mauretania* of 1907, equipped with four sets of turbines, retained the Atlantic speed record for twenty-two years (becoming faster as she grew older, a phenomenom peculiar to some ships).

Today it is pointless and uneconomic to reduce an Atlantic passage by minutes when jets are flying the distance in less than seven hours. The record for the fastest passage stands with the United States Lines' *United States*, which in 1952 crossed from the Ambrose Light to Bishop Rock, a distance of 2,942 miles, in three days ten hours forty minutes at 35.59 knots, returning on a course of 2,902 miles in three days twelve hours twelve minutes at 34.51 knots.

The big passenger ships were always a centre of attention. Their news-value was as great as their size, and they had only to lose an anchor to make the front

page. In size they have been surpassed by the oil tanker. Tankers, and their close relation the bulk-grain or ore carrier are now among the world's largest ships, carrying upwards of a quarter of a million tons of cargo.

The ancestor of the modern tanker was the *Gluckauf*, built in Britain as long ago as 1886 for the German-American Petroleum Company. There is no mistaking her relationship to the tankers of today, for she had her engines and officers' accommodation aft. In the midst of the general flurry of progress in ship design and machinery, particularly the steam turbine, at the end of the nineteenth century, it is a shock to find the four-masted barque *Brilliant* among the cargo ships built in 1901. She was constructed as an oil carrier, and was among the largest of sailing ships, with a tonnage of 3,765 gross.

The *Gluckauf* and the *Brilliant* make a strange contrast. But a further surprise was in store for contemporary students of oil-tanker design when, in 1903, the largest oil carrier yet, the *Narragansett*, was built in Scotland for the Anglo-American Company. She carried 12,000 tons of oil and her pumps were

powerful enough to discharge her cargo in twelve hours. Outwardly she could have been mistaken for a dry-cargo ship because her engines were amidships; her designers were reluctant to put her machinery aft for fear that her extremely long hull (531 feet) would be weakened. She was, incidentally, longer than her passenger liner contemporary, the Canadian Allan Lines' *Victorian*, the first Atlantic liner to be driven by Parsons' steam turbines.

Giant Atlantic liners such as the German *Imperator* and *Bismarck*, the first ships to exceed 50,000 tons gross, became even larger during the pre-1914 years. In the meantime there came upon the scene a new form of propulsion – the diesel engine, which took its name from Rudolf Diesel, a German engineer who lived from 1858 – 1913. He began by experimenting with pulverized coal to burn in the cylinders of an engine; from this developed an engine using heavy oil, and boilers to raise steam were dispensed with. The first ocean-going diesel-driven ship was the *Selandia*, a cargo ship of 4,930 tons built in 1912. She had no funnel: the exhaust gases from her engines were discharged through the mainmast.

The first *Mauretania*, Atlantic record-holder for twenty-two years, here seen passing down the River Tyne in 1907 to begin her trials.

The upper part of the smokeroom of the Cunard liner *Campania*, built in 1893.

Motor ships grew in size and importance between the wars. On the one hand were fast cross-channel ships such as the Belgian *Prince Baudouin* of 1934, built for the Dover-Ostend route, and which reached a trial speed of 25.25 knots; and on the other hand the Dutch liner *Oranje*, built in 1938 – 9 for the Far East trade. She was a triple-screw ship of 19,850 tons and had a speed of 21 knots.

In both world wars the mercantile marine, while performing its commercial functions, deservedly acquired the title of Merchant Navy. By the nature of both wars the western allies had a great deal to gain from their troop carriers, and the supply ships that kept Britain alive in the face of submarine and surface attack – and from the air as well in 1939 – 45. The convoy system, working on the principle of strength in numbers and protected by screening warships, proved itself in both wars. A lesson learned in the First World War was the value of the standard cargo ship and of the big, fast, high-capacity troop ship. This lesson was applied with success in the Second World War: in the United States in particular, astonishing numbers of Liberty cargo ships were built, as speedily as cars on an assembly line – the total number built to the basic design was in fact 2,880.

Equally, the performance of ships of the carrying capacity of the *Queen Mary* and *Queen Elizabeth* probably shortened the war in Europe, for on many voyages in summer they each carried as many as 15,000 troops. Merchant ships were widely used as hospital ships, store ships, and in the early days of 1940 as armed merchant cruisers, though in the latter case their flimsy hulls were too vulnerable to shells and bombs and they were converted to troop ships.

Ironically, the world economic depression that began in 1929 and continued well into the 1930s coincided with decisions in Europe to build big passenger liners for the North Atlantic trade. In Britain the *Queen Mary* lay on the stocks at Clydebank for two years until work could be restarted. But on the continent of Europe a number of superliners came more rapidly into service: the German ships *Bremen*

The *Selandia*, the first ocean-going diesel-driven ship, built in Copenhagen in 1912 for the East Asiatic Company. She had no funnel, the exhaust gases being discharged through the mainmast.

and *Europa*, the *Rex* and *Conte di Savoia*, from Italy, and the French *Normandie* had all been completed by 1935, some with government aid. Conditions of trade were anything but propitious, but ships have long lives and a policy of wait-and-see would have been unwise. By 1936 the *Queen Mary* had also been completed and there were signs of a revival in shipping.

Again there was the interruption of war; the surviving superliners were the two *Queens*. Of the five continental European ships mentioned in the previous paragraph, only the *Europa* remained afloat; later she became the *Liberté* of the French Line.

The immediate post-war years in the cargo trades were years of replacement. There was a very large question mark poised above the future of the passenger liner. Lost tonnage had to be replaced, and the likely effects of jet air travel assessed. The shipping scene changed. Ships that had been classed as passenger-cargo liners became less numerous, for with continually increasing operating costs it was unrealistic to build a ship that required a large crew (particularly in the catering department) to remain idle while the business of discharging and loading cargo continued for a week or more.

Today a new pattern of ship construction and management has evolved to anticipate technological and commercial development over a ship's lifetime, a period of some twenty-five years. Half a century ago this would not have troubled shipowners. But if one considers that even ten years ago people scoffed at the idea of man landing on the moon before the end of 1970, how much more difficult it is to assess what the next quarter century will bring on the seas.

The dividing lines are as clear as can be. Passenger ships, pure and simple, are equipped for their own seasonal trade when the business is there and are equally fit for leisure cruising anywhere in the world; a shore and ship organization developed to land passengers on the morning of arrival, clean ship, take on a fresh complement of passengers and sail the same day. This is now happening. On the cargo front, the container ship and the hinterland organization that acts as 'back-up' are geared to the economics of more sea time and less port time.

Every day a ship lies at anchor, waiting for a berth to discharge her cargo, is a wasted day. Owners are investing in larger, faster, better-equipped ships. Hence the increase in size and speed of conventional cargo liners, container ships, bulk carriers and oil tankers. A paradox from the past gives a clue. Sir Percy Bates, Chairman of the Cunard Company during the building of the *Queen Mary* and *Queen Elizabeth*, described them as the smallest and slowest ships that could provide a weekly Atlantic service, replace three ships, and make a substantial profit. The 26-knot, 49,340-ton container ships and the 250,000-ton oil tankers of the 1970s prove the economic sense of the big ship in large-scale, long-distance trading.

Nuclear ship propulsion has been an object of public interest for nearly twenty years. Its advantage for warships – a capacity to remain at sea with no worries about refuelling – was and is important. For commercial operation the prospects were less attractive: a greatly increased building cost had to be faced, and increased operating costs as well, compared with a conventionally powered ship. Other deterrents were the weight of the nuclear power plant, with its heavy shield, and the reluctance of some countries to accept nuclear merchant ships in their harbours for fear that radio-active material

1. A famous Atlantic racer of the 1890s, the *Kaiser Wilhelm der Grosse*: she crossed from Sandy Hook Light to the Needles in five days seventeen hours eight minutes.

2. The *Bremen* (1929), a Norddeutscher Lloyd liner: she was the first ship to break the Cunard *Mauretania's* Blue Riband record, which had stood for twenty-two years.

3. The Italian liner *Conte di Savoia* of 1932, one of the first large passenger liners to be equipped with gyro stabilizers.

4. Another prestige ship, the *Rex,* also built in Italy in 1932 for the southern route across the Atlantic. In 1933 she won the Blue Riband by crossing from Gibraltar to the Ambrose Lightship in 4 days 13 hours 58 minutes at an average speed of 28.92 knots.

3

4

might be released if the ship were in a collision. Even so, only by practical experiment can a new and complicated 'prime mover', as the marine engineer describes a set of main engines, be judged. The USA laid the keel of the the world's first nuclear powered merchant ship on 11 May 1958, Mrs Richard Nixon performing the ceremony. The ship was launched on 21 July 1959 by Mrs Dwight D. Eisenhower, and named *Savannah*, after the Atlantic pioneer of 1819.

The *Savannah* was ready for sea in 1962. She displaces 20,000 tons; her cargo capacity is 9,300 tons and her 22,000 horsepower machinery drives her at 21 knots. In essence the *Savannah* has been a floating nuclear test-bed. A typical year of commercial operation, from August 1966 to August 1967, was revealed in figures in a report of the American Maritime Ad-

ministration. The *Savannah* had covered 86,000 miles on voyages to Europe, called at seventy-four ports and carried 36,000 tons of cargo. Operating costs were the nub: $3,909,681 compared with freight income of $2,614,421. Elsewhere, a German nuclear merchant ship, the *Otto Hahn,* an iron ore carrier, has been in service since 1969. Russia commissioned the world's first nuclear-powered surface ship, the icebreaker *Lenin,* in December 1959; she has since been claimed as a great success. Japan has a nuclear merchant ship at sea, an experimental cargo ship of modest dimensions capable of carrying 2,400 tons at sixteen knots. She was launched in June 1969 with the name *Mutsu*. Designs have been worked out in Britain for a 40,000-ton container ship; at the time of writing these were being studied by the government.

A classic picture. The *Queen Mary* is seen arriving at Southampton in August 1946 at the end of her war career as a troopship. Beside her the *Queen Elizabeth* is making ready for her maiden commercial voyage, which began on 16th October 1946.

The French liner *Normandie* arriving at Plymouth, England in June 1935 after breaking all records for a trans-Atlantic crossing; her speed on this run was such that her hull became stripped of its paint.

The *Empress of Britain,* flagship of the Canadian Pacific fleet in the late 1930s. She carried King George VI and Queen Elizabeth to Canada in 1939, and was destroyed by torpedo in 1940.

It is difficult to predict the future of nuclear power in ships built to earn their keep and make a profit by carrying passengers and cargo, but it is not unreasonable to say that a breakthrough will come. At present the weight of a nuclear power plant absorbs an excessive amount of revenue-earning capacity compared with a conventional cargo ship. Also to be considered is that at present a nuclear reactor, in its cycle of activity, offers a comprehensive service: it first produces heat; this raises steam in special boilers and is used to drive the main engines – steam turbines – and also to drive auxiliary turbo-genertators, which provide light and heat.

Many theoretical studies have been made of the future of nuclear-powered commercial ships. They are far-ranging. A submarine cargo carrier; an articulated cargo ship embodying a nuclear 'pusher' unit that could be detached on arrival at a terminal port and be re-coupled to an already fully-loaded cargo section, thus speeding up turn-round time; a closed-cycle gas turbine using helium under com-

The Japanese experimental nuclear-powered merchant ship *Mutsu*. She has a length of 426 feet and a cargo capacity of 2,400 tons; her nuclear reactor provides 10,000 horsepower for a speed of $16\frac{1}{2}$ knots.

The *United States,* the fastest and most powerful passenger liner ever built; on her maiden voyage in 1952 she broke the Atlantic record at an average speed of 34.48 knots.

The transverse construction of a bulk carrier of the 1970s; notable features include the bulb bow and rapidly broadening hull form.

The *Atherstone,* a bulk carrier of advanced design built in Japan in 1965. The ship has a cargo capacity (43,965 tons deadweight) and is powered by a diesel engine of modest horsepower (14,700) which gives an economical speed of fifteen knots.

pression, heated in a nuclear reactor to well over 1,000 degrees Fahrenheit, and then passed through turbines to drive the propeller shaft. Apart from safety of operation, which is vital, there are two associated factors: reduction in the cost of nuclear fuel, and capital cost of machinery. It thus suggests application to big, high-powered, high-speed cargo carriers. The result would be an increase in the number of voyages these could make in a single year, always providing that world trading demand maintained their load factors well above break-even point and so produced profits.

The liner today

Hamburg, West Germany, 25,002 tons gross (1969)

There follows a look at some of today's notable deep-sea passenger liners, some designed in the 1960s for the dual purpose of regular service and cruising, others towards the end of the decade, created from the keel upwards as leisure ships. In either employment, the principle is that of the hotel resort that moves. Ship design and engineering techniques today are capable of producing ships of vast size and speed for passenger employment (as indeed they have in the case of the monster oil tankers and bulk carriers) but the first consideration is public demand. And the key questions are initial cost, operational costs in an inflationary environment, present and future markets, and, most important of all, profit potential. Will each new passenger ship, with allowance for modification and improvement, be profitable during her expected life of twenty-five years? Shipowners, internationally, are investing in new liners ships because they believe they have a profitable future—when they are tailor-made for their purpose.

Rotterdam, Holland (1959)

In appearance the *Rotterdam* breaks with convention, dispensing with funnels; these are replaced by twin 'pipes' abreast that are balanced by a structure that is more fore-top than mast. The *Rotterdam* was designed for the dual purpose of trans-atlantic liner and cruise ship, with no pretensions to speed. She is thus economical on fuel. Aluminium alloy reduces the top-weight of the superstructure. The *Rotterdam* broke new ground in passenger liner design in that her accommodation is arranged lengthwise rather than vertically, which gives a more balanced allocation of space.

Tonnage, 38,645 tons gross; length, 748 feet; breadth, 94 feet; machinery, double reduction geared turbines developing 20,000 horsepower; speed, 20.5 knots.

Windsor Castle, Great Britain (1960)

The *Windsor Castle* is the largest liner on the Britain-South Africa route. She was launched by Her Majesty

France, France, 66,348 tons
gross (1961)

Following spread:
Queen Elizabeth II, Great
Britain, 65,864 tons gross
(1968)

Queen Elizabeth the Queen Mother from the Cammel Laird shipyard in Birkenhead, Cheshire, on 22 June 1959. When she sailed on her maiden voyage on 18 August 1960 her speed cut the passage from Southampton to Cape Town from 13½ to 11½ days.

Tonnage, 36,123 tons gross; length, 783 feet; breadth, 92 feet; machinery, geared turbines developing 49,400 horsepowers; speed, 22.5 knots.

Canberra, Great Britain (1961)

Here is another example of design innovation in passenger liners. The *Canberra* was built at Belfast by Harland & Wolff in 1961 at a cost of fifteen million pounds. She was the largest passenger liner to be built in Britain since the *Queen Elizabeth* in 1938. By putting the machinery right aft, space was opened for more spacious passenger accomodation, unbroken by funnel uptakes. Additional sun-deck space for recreation, also reduction in weight topsides, was achieved by placing lifeboats, davits, and winches on a lower deck.

Tonnage, 44,807 tons gross; length, 818.5 feet; breadth, 102 feet; machinery, steam turbines developing 88,200 horsepower; speed, 26.5 knots.

France, France (1961)

The longest liner in the world. Distinctive features are the wings on the funnels to keep the decks free from smuts. The accomodation for first- and tourist-class passengers is decorated with the taste of the best French post-war design. The *France* was built to operate a five-day Atlantic service from Le Havre and Southampton to New York and to include cruising as part of her work. She reached a trial speed of 34.15 knots (exceeded only by the American liner *United States*).

Tonnage, 66,348 tons gross; length, 1,035 feet; breadth, 110.7 feet; machinery, single reduction geared turbines developing 157,800 horsepower; speed, 31 knots.

Michelangelo and Raffaello, Italy (1965)

These two remarkable ships are the pride of the Italian passenger fleet. They were built for the Mediterrean to New York service of Italia, or the Italian Line, with cruising an important element in their operation. External novelties are the lattice-work funnels with flat tops, adopted after wind-tunnel tests to determine the most efficient means of dispersing smoke and smuts. The *Michelangelo* was launched on 16 September 1962 and began her maiden voyage to New York on 12 May 1965. Tonnage, 45,911 tons gross; length, 904 feet; breadth, 102 feet; machinery, steam turbines developing 87,000 horsepower; speed, $26\frac{1}{2}$ knots.

Oceanic, Greece (1965)

The *Oceanic's* service was to have been a Mediterranean route to New York. She was designed during the transitional period when air competition was threatening ships of her size – halfway between an intermediate passenger liner and a superliner. Her owners judged that as a single unit she could not be operated profitably on the regular Atlantic route. They fitted her in to the developing American market

Oceanic, Greece, 27,644 tons gross (1965)

Cunard Adventurer, Great Britain, 15,000 tons gross (1971)

for the leisure ship sailing from New York to Nassau. Tonnage, 27,644 tons gross; length, 782 feet; breadth, 96.7 feet; machinery, steam turbines developing 60,500 horsepower; speed, 26.5 knots.

Queen Elizabeth II, Great Britain (1968)

Britain's most notable post-war passenger liner. Built at a time when Atlantic airlines had captured the passenger market, her design had to fulfil the twin requirements of the five-day Atlantic service in the summer season, and of world-wide cruising. With the most powerful twin-screw machinery ever installed in a passenger liner she can achieve 28.5 knots on a daily fuel consumption of only 500 tons of oil, compared with the 1,000 tons of the earlier Cunard *Queens.* She has only three main boilers compared with the twenty-four of the *Queen Mary* and the twelve of the *Queen Elizabeth.*

Tonnage, 65,864 tons gross; length, 963 feet; breadth, 105 feet; machinery, double reduction geared turbines developing 110,000 horsepower; speed, 28.5 knots.

Hamburg, West Germany (1969)

The *Hamburg* was designed in Germany to carry 600 passengers for Atlantic and cruising service. She has the modern bulb bow, to improve her speed and

reduce pitching. There is a wide use of glass in the superstructure to provide maximum light. Conventions in the funnel design of today's passenger liners have combined to drop the straight-up-and-down stack; the *Hamburg's* funnel can be compared with the latticework structures of the Italian liners *Michelangelo* and *Raffaello,* in that it is surmounted by a flat-top device to keep the passenger decks free from the pollution of smoke and soot.

Tonnage, 25,002 tons gross; length, 644 feet; breadth, 90 feet; machinery, steam turbines developing 23,000 horsepower; speed, 22 knots.

Cunard Adventurer, Great Britain (1971)

Another interpretation of the cruise liner, designed primarily for short cruises, averaging twelve days, from New York to the Caribbean. Again there is emphasis on deck space and on an observation point for passengers. The *Cunard Adventurer* was built in Rotterdam, designed in Copenhagen, and her passenger accommodation was planned in New York — a truly international collaboration. In common with other modern cruise ships the *Cunard Adventurer* is fully air-conditioned and is fitted with anti-rolling stabilizers.

Tonnage, 15,000 tons gross; length, 484 feet; breadth, 71 feet; machinery, four Stork-Werkspoor 12 cylinder diesel engines developing 26,800 horsepower driving twin screws; speed, $20\frac{1}{2}$ knots.

Nordic Prince, Norway (1971)

The *Nordic Prince,* and her sister ship *Song of Norway* each with a passenger capacity of 870, were built in Finland for the American cruise market, based on Miami, Florida, their cruise itineraries including ports in the Caribbean. Apart from expected cruise liner features such as full air-conditioning, stabilizers and all cabins equipped with showers, these ships include an observation 'post' located in the outside of the funnel casing, the nearest yet to passengers having a view from the crow's nest. Diesel propelling machinery is installed, and the funnel is so designed that what engine exhaust there is will be dispersed well-clear of passenger space.

Tonnage, 18,400 tons gross; length, 552 feet; breadth, 78.7 feet; machinery, four diesel engines developing 18,000 horsepower; speed, 21 knots.

Spirit of London, Great Britain (1972)

This is an example of the smaller custom-built cruise liner. A ship of 15,000 tons, modest in size but accommodating 750 passengers in 409 cabins, equipped with multi-channel radios and telephones. The bridge and wheelhouse are placed below the observation lounge, giving passengers a better viewpoint when the ship enters port. This impression below was done in the early days of planning. During the building of the ship further studies revealed areas for improvement. Her base is San Francisco.

Tonnage, 15,000 tons gross; length, 535 feet; breadth, 75 feet; machinery, four diesel engines developing 18,000 horsepower; speed, 20.5 knots.

Freaks

Anton Flettner's rotor ship *Barbara,* built in Germany in 1925.

The *Armenia,* a Hudson River craft notable for her tall funnel and 'walking-beam' engine.

Strange ships have appeared on the seas throughout the history of merchant and fighting ships; some of their designers were cranks obsessed with impractical proposals, which they persuaded wealthy and eccentric men to sponsor. For all that, the history of the mechanically propelled ship follows a logical line of development. More became known about the potential power of steam and of the property of metals under the stress of extreme heat – the outcome is today's steam turbine fed with steam at very high pressures and temperatures. The heavy oil, or diesel engine has developed in step. And nuclear power applied to ships is under practical and theoretical study.

Flettner's Rotor Ship
Harnessing the Wind

Despite the rapid progress made in recent years to create energy by mechanical and technological means, the greater part of the history of the ship occupies centuries when man had nothing but the natural force and direction of the winds to propel his ships across the oceans; and the sailing ship reached its apogee in the clipper ship. Today sails, sailing and the winds serve leisure before commerce.

Yet there was a serious attempt between the wars to harness the winds to add power to a ship while dispensing with sails. The man behind the theory was a German engineer, Anton Flettner, who first experimented and then secured financial support from the German government to convert one of a type of small cargo vessel to what he called a rotor ship. His ship, *Barbara,* was driven by diesel engines of 1,000 horsepower. With engines only, the *Barbara* made nine knots. Now comes the grotesque aspect of Flettner's invention of rotors. They were huge light-alloy towers, fifty-five feet high and thirteen feet in diameter, each with a delicately balanced revolving core that was spun clockwise or anti-clockwise by the force of the wind. In Flettner's assessment they were a more efficient substitute for sails, acting as an auxiliary to give more speed, without increasing the horsepower and fuel consumption of her main engine.

In a fair wind the rotors alone gave the *Barbara* a speed of six knots; used in conjunction with the engines the ship reached thirteen knots. This was by no means an impressive performance; Flettner's idea, the revival of the sailing ship in a new shape, was in practice still-born. His theories had no commercial future because interest continued to centre round

The freak to beat all freaks, the *Connector,* a ship built in three hinged sections.

engines; and these were in a state of constant change and refinement – providing more power, consuming less fuel, they were becoming cheaper to build and cheaper to maintain.

Armenia (1849)
The Walking Steamboat

If, in 1849, a stranger picked the right moment to stand on the banks of the Hudson River, a few miles above New York, he would have seen an extraordinary craft steaming up river. She had a very low freeboard, or, put a different way, appeared to sit so low in the water that a passenger could have leaned over the side and washed his hands in the river. She had a very tall funnel, painted black like a stove pipe, and enormous paddle-boxes. She was the *Armenia*, built in 1849 to operate a ferry service from New York to places far up the Hudson.

The features so far described were not in themselves unusual in a river steamboat. But our stranger would have been astonished by what seemed to be a huge iron see-saw, supported by a stout diamond-shaped framework sticking twenty-five feet or more above the top deck. The see-saw performed a fascinating rocking motion, which continued until the

ship was brought to a stop. It was what was known as a 'walking-beam' engine, a colourful name because it suggests that the *Armenia* was actually walking on the river.

This type of machinery never caught on in Europe. It had advantages on the long American rivers, particularly in stretches of shallow water. The engineers were not restricted in the length of piston stroke – in the *Armenia* it was as much as fourteen feet – and the movement of the beam could be transmitted to paddle-wheels of tremendous size, producing a fair turn of speed.

To European eyes the *Armenia* would have appeared to be a freak, but she was a practical freak. To put the size of the *Armenia*'s forty-foot diameter paddle-wheels into perspective – and they were fitted in a small hull – they were of equal diameter to those of the Cunard liner *Persia* (built in 1856) which was the largest ship in the world at the time of her completion. The difference was that in an ocean-going ship engineers were obliged to put the machinery well down in the hull to give maximum stability in heavy weather. Nonetheless there is no reason why the 'walking-beam' could not have been used in river boats on some of the long rivers in Asia.

117

The elaborately decorated interior of Bessemer's 'floating saloon'.

The Connector (c 1850) of the Jointed Ship Company, Rood Lane, London

The very name of her owners questions the sanity of the men who put up the money to build this freak ship to end all freak ships. Undoubtedly the *Connector* was built, but precisely *when* is a puzzle. One reads that she was built about 1850; that it was 1858 in the Joyce shipyard at Greenwich; that it was 1863 at Blackwall. But it is certain that she made a trip down the Thames to Erith Reach, which could be defined as acceptance trials.

There is doubt whether she was built in four sections or in three; possibly a fourth was added later. Contemporary impressions of the *Connector* credit her with three hinged sections. The object of the hinges was to help the ship to ride easier in a rough sea, with no risk of breaking her back, because the hinges would undulate the sections to the motion of the waves. It was also claimed that time would be saved in loading and discharging cargo. The sections would be unhinged and towed to convenient cargo berths in the docks.

The *Connector*'s commercial purpose was to carry coal from Newcastle to London, not the other way round, as one would imagine in a project so fanciful. How many voyages the *Connector* made is not revealed. The most that can be said is that the designers at least gave her an iron hull with propeller-driven machinery. But how her sections were connected and

disconnected is mystery, and it is significant that news of her fate did not reach the general public.

The Great Eastern (1858)
Isambard Kingdom Brunel's Magnificent Failure

There is something special about the concept of this extraordinary ship. Her statistics were larger than life – quite suitable in an England about a third of the way through Queen Victoria's reign. Earlier we described the P & O liner *Himalaya* (1853) as one of the largest of her day: she was 340 feet long; her tonnage was 3,438. The *Great Eastern*, laid down a year later, was twice the *Himalaya*'s length and more than five times her tonnage. It was as if the Empire State Building in New York had been ousted a year after it was built by a monster skyscraper of 204 storeys and a height of 2,944 feet.

In the *Great Eastern* there was space for 4,000 paying passengers or 10,000 troops less favourably accommodated. She could carry 6,000 tons of cargo and 12,000 tons of coal for fuel. She was a nineteenth-century floating coal mine. Why so much coal? This huge capacity was the raison d'être of the ship. The theory was that she could carry 4,000 passengers and 6,000 tons of cargo to Australia without calling at expensive depots that would have had to be stocked with coal. Likewise she could steam to India and back without refuelling. Had she taken up this service she might well have been a success.

The enterprise of the 'Great Ship' was proposed in 1851 when Isambard Kingdom Brunel was consultant engineer to the Eastern Steam Navigation Company. Brunel's plan was to build one very large ship to take the place of a fleet of small ships. In this alone he was seventy-five years ahead of his time. When the technology of naval architecture, marine engineering and ship management were equal to the task 80,000-ton, $28\frac{1}{2}$-knot ships, notably the *Queen Mary* and *Queen Elizabeth*, replaced an Atlantic express service that had required three ships. But back in 1858, the *Great Eastern* was too big and underpowered for any man

The true size of the *Great Eastern* is brought home in this contemporary record of the first attempt made to launch her. After her owners had been trying for three months to get the great ship into the Thames, she eventually slid into the water unaided.

to handle, whether managing director, captain or chief engineer.

The *Great Eastern* lacked nothing in the strength of her hull. Brunel and his co-designer, Scott Russell, produced a stout, well-shaped structure that could take punishment without showing signs of fracture. But the combination of screw propeller, paddle wheels, and a full rig of sail, on paper the most practical means of driving this great ship, did not amount in sheer horsepower to what this mass of inert iron required if it was to be given direction and course.

Trouble was always in step with the *Great Eastern* whatever she did or wherever she went. She consumed hundreds of thousands of pounds. She so worried Brunel that he had a stroke which killed him. At her launch, sideways into the Thames, on 3 November 1857, she moved a few feet and stuck fast.

Three months at a cost of £120,000, which was ten times Brunel's estimate, were spent in attempts to launch her. Eventually she launched herself, slipping gently into the river on 31 January 1858. But by then she had bankrupted her owners.

Nearly two years after her launch the *Great Eastern* was still at anchor in the Thames awaiting a buyer. The Great Ship Company bought her for £160,000, a quarter of her building cost. On a trial trip in September 1859, an explosion in one of her two engine rooms killed six firemen. With no trade in prospect she wintered in Southampton. Her first commander, Captain Harrison, was drowned when a launch taking him ashore overturned.

The *Great Eastern* put to sea on her maiden voyage in June 1860. She arrived at New York eleven days and two hours later. She was described as the ugliest thing that had ever sailed the seas. At the foot of

Sir William Bessemer's cross-channel boat of 1875, fitted with a gimbal-mounted saloon that was designed to banish sea-sickness; it was a failure.

Manhattan, thousands crowded the Battery shoreline. Guns were set off; the bells of Trinity Church played 'Rule Britannia.' In five days 143,764 people paid fifty cents apiece to inspect the largest ship in the world.

Interest in her soon waned. She made a series of Atlantic voyages, disastrous financially and disastrous in the damage she suffered from Atlantic weather at its worst. She was stout enough to stay afloat but her machinery was too feeble to control her. She left a trail of debts behind her; even a lottery failed, for there were not enough people willing to pay £1 for a ticket. In 1865 and 1866 there was a respite from misfortune. The *Great Eastern* successfully laid five trans-Atlantic cable lines. In 1870 she rounded the Cape of Good Hope with 4,000 miles of telegraph cable and an enormous quantity of coal; in this she very nearly exceeded her own statistics, for the deadweight of cable and coal was 15,835 tons.

She successfully laid the Bombay-to-Aden stretch of cable-link to Europe. She was then laid up for eleven years, and suffered the indignity of becoming a floating amusement park with huge advertising slogans painted on her sides. She went to the scrap heap in 1888.

The strength of her hull must have been phenomenal for it took three years to demolish it. When the shipbreakers reached the double bottom it is said that in one of the compartments they found the skeleton of a man, presumably sealed-in during the early stages of building. Immediately the superstitious were presented with a reason for the calamitous life of the *Great Eastern*.

The Bessemer (1875)
The Ship To End Seasickness

Sir Henry Bessemer was one of those fortunate men born with an inventive and inquiring mind, combining an appreciation of what is practical with what might be achieved by persistence. His name in history is associated with the process he devised in 1856 to convert iron into steel. The persistent side of his nature was occupied in a search for something to banish travel sickness—in his case, sea-sickness. He was what

used to be described as a bad sailor. Today, there are simple medical means to overcome the problem, and modern stabilizers have reduced rolling to negligible proportions.

Bessemer had the financial means to experiment. He sought a design for a public room, or saloon as it was called in Victorian times, which would remain upright, independent of the motion of a ship. In his own back garden he built a scaled-down section of a ship, with a steam-driven donkey engine to simulate motion, allowing for a roll of thirty degrees from one side to the other. He then installed in the model a room mounted on gimbals, working on the same principle as a ship's standard compass, which remains level whatever the motion of the vessel. There was this difference: an additional quartermaster, whose normal duty was to steer the ship, would be detailed to operate a hydraulic mechanism, using a spirit level as a guide, to keep the saloon on an even keel. Bessemer did not pretend that his invention would cure the pitching of a ship; for that he relied on a design of hull that had very little freeboard (height above the

level of the sea) at either end.

There was also the problem of what to do with the machinery if its usual place amidships was occupied by a saloon, ninety feet long and weighing 180 tons. The answer was two engine rooms and two sets of paddle-wheels, with the saloon in the middle; access to other parts of the ship was by flexible gangways, which worked on much the same principle as the modern links between railway carriages.

After months of experiment – Bessemer did not do things by halves – the Bessemer Saloon Ship Company was launched and the ship, *Bessemer*, 350 feet long, with engines of 4,600 horsepower giving a speed of sixteen knots, was built on the River Humber in 1875.

The *Bessemer* was completed, made several crossings between Dover and Calais with scientists, shipbuilders, and the press as guests, but the anti-rolling saloon was never tried out in conditions of rough seas. So much effort for so little result. The *Bessemer* had been announced to the public as the ship with the steady saloon that banished sea-sickness. But it was not working, and the *Bessemer*'s outward ap-

The Obelisk ship *Cleopatra* at Westminster Bridge on her arrival from Egypt.

pearance did not invite confidence – in one ungrammatical phrase 'she looked so un-ship like'. In 1876 the *Bessemer*, unwanted as a passenger carrier, returned to her builders and was converted into a cargo ship, only to be wrecked on the east coast on her first trip to London.

Cleopatra (1877)
The Needle Ship

In Egypt in a temple at Deir-el-Bahari near Thebes there are wall sculptures showing two enormous obelisks – each at least 100 feet long and probably weighing 700 tons – making their way down the Nile in a giant boat. How they were put afloat, and how far advanced in the techniques of boat-building were the Egyptians of Queen Hatshepsut's day, around 1500 BC, is a subject for wonder.

More than 3,300 years later the Victorians in England were faced with the problem of how to ship to London an obelisk, known as Cleopatra's Needle, from the bed of sand near Alexandria where it had lain since Augustus had attempted to move it to Rome in 23 BC. It was then fashionable for capital cities to acquire an obelisk or needle from Egypt. In 1836 the French shipped a 240-ton obelisk to Paris, where it stands in the Place de la Concorde. Then, two years after Cleopatra's Needle was erected on the Victoria Embankment in London, a similar monolith, also given the name of Cleopatra's Needle, crossed the

Atlantic in a ship called the *Dessoug* to New York, and was given a home in Central Park.

The London Cleopatra's Needle weighed about 185 tons and was sixty-eight and a half feet high. Engineers devised a cylindrical iron boat with a length of ninety-three feet and a diameter of fifteen feet. They christened it *Cleopatra*, built a small deckhouse for a crew, provided a catwalk, a single mast, and a simple rudder controlled from the deckhouse. Captain Henry Carter, who supervised the equipping of the *Cleopatra*, had to endure several mishaps, and false 'launches', until he was satified that the extraordinary ship he was to command was fit for sea. In tow of a small steamer, the *Olga*, commanded by a Captain Booth, and at the end of 400 yards of steel cable, the *Cleopatra* left Alexandria on 21 September 1877, with a crew of eight.

The Mediterranean passage was smooth but the *Cleopatra* was an abominable craft to handle. The little convoy was abreast of Cape Finisterre when the Bay of Biscay lived up to its name as the Bay of storms. Conditions were so bad, threatening both ships, that Captain Carter cast off the towline; the Olga sent a boat across with six men to rescue Carter and his crew. It was close alongside the *Cleopatra* when a vicious sea swept it away. The *Cleopatra*'s condition was desperate. In the morning Captain Carter and his Maltese crew managed to board the *Olga* and the *Cleopatra* was abandoned.

This was not the end of the story. Luckily, the *Cleopatra* was taken in tow by a passing steamer and berthed in Ferrol in north-west Spain. There she lay until the tug *Anglia* came out from England, in January 1878, to tow her to London. Four months after leaving Egypt the Obelisk boat was safely moored off St Thomas's Hospital, where she became the curiosity of London and a source of income to Thames boatmen until the Needle was set upright on 12 September 1878. Underneath it were laid an assortment of memorabilia, from a portrait of Queen Victoria to a copy of Bradshaw's Railway Guide and a set of British coins.

Special purpose ships

The 195,900-ton Shell tanker *Marinula*. She is strictly a functional ship; for all the mathematical precision of her hull shape from stern to bows, viewed from this angle her hull form has a certain beauty of line.

The *Admiral*, the twentieth century successor to the *Mississippi*, presents an altogether different appearance. The shallow draught is there, and the castellated superstructure, but for all her 4,000 capacity she is out of touch with the history of the river – perhaps someone may be found in the United States to build a replica of a boat such as the *Natchez* and recreate profitably an old-style Mississippi 'racer'.

River navigation is not the pedestrian operation it might seem, nor does it require unimaginatively designed craft. When one considers the great rivers, their length, their width and varying depths of water, they assume the proportions of oceans. The Mississippi from the Gulf of Mexico to its confluence with the Missouri is 1,192 miles long. The Missouri itself extends for 2,908 miles. Together the two waterways stretch for over 4,000 miles through some of the richest territory in the USA.

The rivers, legendary in themselves and in the history of their country, gave rise to a type of boat that has had no equal anywhere in the world. It was Robert Fulton, designer of the pioneer steamboat *Clermont* who brought steam to the Mississippi in 1811 with a side-wheeler, the *New Orleans*. Mark Twain spread the romance and the fantasy of the Mississippi steamboats, not only by word-spinning but from experience as well. As a young man Mark Twain worked in the steamboats and became a pilot. Apart from commerce the steamboats of the river were given another role as entertainers, becoming the showboats of the 1870s that have been the stars of more than one romantic film.

A superstructure like a house of cards, enormous stern paddles and twin stovepipe funnels pouring out so much thick black smoke that it seemed they would burst – such were the unworldly qualities of these ungainly but practical craft. They were elaborately decorated with scrollwork and gilding. The passenger accommodation was adorned with oil paintings, intricately carved woodwork, velvet curtains and chandeliers, a combination of ostentation and vulgarity that today has a fascination.

Legends grew from the fever for river racing. Funnels poured out showers of sparks and became red hot; boilers had their safety valves sealed down; there were many explosions wrecking entire boats. One blew up with such violence that a boiler was shot into the air, to land in a Cincinnati street. The greatest race was between the *Natchez* and the *Robert E. Lee* in 1870, from New Orleans to St Louis over a distance

of 1,218 miles. Hundreds of thousands of dollars were placed as bets. The *Natchez* under the command of Captain Thomas P. Leathers had set a record of three days twenty-one hours fifty-eight minutes that inflamed Captain John W. Cannon of the *Robert E. Lee*. He stripped his boat to lighten her, recklessly rejected cargo and passengers and went to the lengths of placing coal barges at points on the river. He sailed five minutes ahead of the *Natchez*, which had her usual complement of passengers and cargo. For miles they raced neck-a-neck. The *Robert E. Lee* stopped at her barge stations; the *Natchez* bunkered from the shore but later also resorted to barges. At the end the

Robert E. Lee made the distance in three days eighteen hours thirty minutes, with the *Natchez* more than six hours behind. But many of the bets were cancelled because of Captain Cannon's unfair advantage.

Today the river's excursion boats are streamlined floating hotels. But the true commercial successor to the Mississippi boat is the pushboat, which pushes whole strings of barges laden with thousands of tons of cargo, from oil, coal, gravel and grain to rocket parts. A pushboat has depth-sounders, radar and radio telephones, and has charge of as much valuable cargo as would be carried in an ocean-going ship.

The American Waterways Operators Association, based in Washington, represents the interests of American barge and towing operators. In our brief view of American waterways, emphasis has been on the Mississippi and Missouri Rivers, with all the emotional appeal of the sternwheelers. Today the economic potential of American waterways in terms of the movement of cargoes has come to the forefront. There are statistics of every kind to prove the point. The most important are at that present 4,250 towboats and tugs handle 18,000 barges, which move fifteen per cent of American domestic commerce over a distance of more than 25,000 miles of inland navigation channels.

A stern-wheel American river boat, the *Mississippi,* moored at Hannibal, Missouri, on the Mississippi River; a romantic boat from the last century.

The *Delta Queen*. She was assembled in a Clyde shipyard in Scotland; her parts were put together in Stockton, California in 1926 and she was employed on an overnight service between Sacramento and San Francisco. After war service she found her way back to her natural habitat – the Mississippi.

The *Kowloon Bay,* an example of today's multi-purpose container ship; her cargo might include anything from machinery parts to meat and butter in refrigerated spaces.

The principle of roll-on/roll-off applied to long distance carriers. Notice the attention to the intricacies of cargo handling and stowage throughout this ship, the *Paralla* (this applies equally to her sister ships, *Allunga* and *Dilkara*).

The *Irfon* (1971), a ship that has three identities: as an oil tanker, a bulk carrier, conveying grain or bauxite, and as an ore carrier loaded with iron ore.

A ship of the mid-1970s: the liquefied natural gas carrier, her protective 'domes' suggesting a moon vehicle rather than a ship.

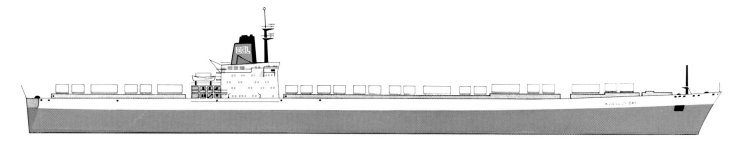

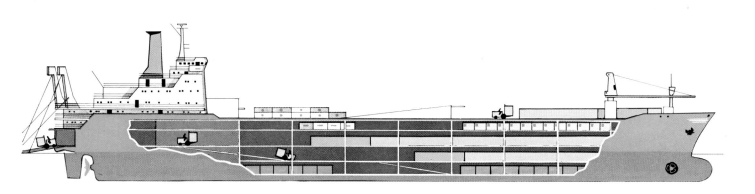

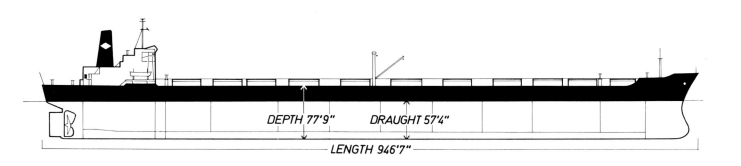

DEPTH 77'9"   DRAUGHT 57'4"

— LENGTH 946'7" —

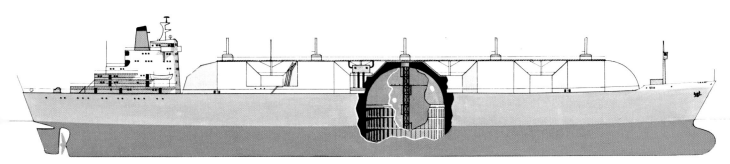

Fully-loaded with nearly a quarter of a million tons of oil, the *Esso Cambria* thrusts through the sea at sixteen knots; bulk, breadth and sheer size are conveyed in this striking picture of a big tanker in action.

A 'pushboat' of the Mississippi today, showing the square bow used to thrust before her a string of heavily laden barges. There could be no greater contrast than this boat and the old stern-wheelers.

The Giant Oil Tanker

The carriage of oil in specialized power-driven ships covers a period of eighty-five years, from the 2,307-ton *Gluckauf* to today's 250,000-ton ships and tomorrow's ships of half a million tons. In between came light relief – the horse and cart of the Atlantic. In 1907 there was built the *Iroquois*, the first twin-screw oil tanker with her machinery installed aft, as in the *Gluckauf*. The *Iroquois* was the horse. The cart was a six-masted schooner-rigged sailing barge named the *Navahoe*. Between them the two ships could carry 18,000 tons of oil, the *Navahoe* travelling at the end of a towline.

Immediately before the Second World War, the size of tankers was averaging about 14,000 tons deadweight. But the post-war demand for oil, coupled with advanced technology in the design and size of ships, gradually made it possible to build tankers of upwards of 200,000 tons capacity. Their advantage is that they carry a vast quantity of oil on a single voyage; and the crew required is insignificant in number compared with the value of the load. A 250,000-ton tanker has a crew of thirty-five. The disadvantage is that ships of this size are limited in the number of ports with water deep enough to receive them – hence the construction of tanker terminals, ideally as close as possible to refineries. The big tankers need more than sixty-five feet of water under their keels. The *France,* the longest passenger liner in the world, measures 1,035 feet. A typical 250,000-ton tanker is the *Esso Northumbria* (1969). She is 1,141 feet long and her breadth is a staggering 170 feet, equalling the length of many coasters and ferries.

Finally, in contrast, let us look at the carrying of oil and liquid in the distant past. In China, about 1700, Newchwang junks, specially caulked and internally sub-divided, carried fifty tons of water in bulk. Oil was also carried down the Irawadi River in Burma to Rangoon in native boats. In 1795 there was built for an Isle of Man owner a sailing ship, the *Ramsey,* equipped with tanks. The 19th century saw a sailing ship named the *Charles* carrying crude oil across the Atlantic until she was destroyed by fire in 1872. In Russia, the Nobel Brothers devised craft to carry crude oil on the River Volga and also across the Caspian Sea. Oil in barrels, known as case oil, was also carried early in the present century in specially adapted sailing ships.

The *Benlawers* at speed.
Notice her massive swinging
derricks, capable of handling
heavy lifts of upwards of
twenty tons.

The Conventional Cargo Liner of the 1970s

The *Benlawers,* a typical cargo liner, was built on the Clyde for the Far East services of the Ben Line, a long-established Scottish shipping company, whose ships include in their itineraries Hong Kong, Manila, Pusan, Yokohama, Nagoya and Kobe. She began her maiden voyage on 27 June 1970. In designing a vessel of this size and type in the age of container ships, versatility in cargo facilities and operation were major factors. The *Benlawers* has four main hatches, side-loading doors, four 'tween-decks in the main holds, each deck, including the lower hold, serviced by electrically operated pallet elevators. Her massive swinging derricks help speed loading and discharge of cargo. There are two compartments that can take 85 cars; and there is space for 192 containers, 135 underdeck and 57 on deck. The *Benlawers,* a single-screw motor ship driven by a 26,100-bhp Sulzer diesel engine, has a service speed of $21\frac{1}{2}$ knots. She is 600 feet in length and has a cubic capacity for cargo of over one million feet, corresponding to a deadweight tonnage of 14,900 tons. It must be remembered that all cargo cannot be containerized. Oil and grain in bulk are examples. Besides, there is a whole family of specialized ships from car ferries to cable layers.

The Container Ship

The container ship was developed to overcome problems of conventional cargo ship operation. These included the loading and discharging costs of cargo of all kinds at the various ports of destination; the distribution of weight; the prevalance of pilfering during loading and discharge. Container ships taking on board thousands of large-scale boxes, each with its own intact content, perhaps cases of whisky, machine parts, or complete items of domestic equipment from refrigerators to food mixers, demand an equally sophisticated harbour 'back-up'. There is the equivalent of a railway marshalling yard where the containers can be separated and disposed for the ships awaiting them. There is conveyance to the port. And the most elaborate equipment has been devised

to load containers over travelling gantries, the root of the operation to save time and get a ship away to sea in a minimum period of port time. Container ships do not displace bulk carriers, such as oil tankers and ore carriers, nor are many ports in the world equipped to handle them. But they show how the shipping industry is ready to adapt itself to new ideas.

Overseas Containers Limited is a British group that in 1966 designed a class of ship for the Europe – Australia trade. Its latest development has been a number of ships designed for the Far East trade, with the consideration that they could conceivably be routed through the Panama Canal – automatically limiting their dimensions. Within these design criteria has

been produced a remarkable compression of carrying capacity and size. The *Liverpool Bay* and her sister ships are almost as long as the *Queen Elizabeth II*. With machinery of 80,000 horse power they have a speed of twenty-six knots. They carry 2,300 containers, amounting to a deadweight of 34,000 tons.

The Roll-on/Roll-off Container Ship

Three ships for the USA – Australia cargo service provide an interesting variation in container ship design. They are named *Paralla*, *Allunga*, and *Dilkara*, all completed in 1971. This is a truly international venture, the participants being Australian, British and Swedish. Each of the ships flies the mer-

chant ship flag of one of the three countries. The combined interests form the Pacific Australia Direct Line, registered as PAD Australia Proprietary Limited.

Versatility in operation is an important aspect of the design of these ships. With building and operating costs accelerating, and considering that a ship's life averages twenty-five years, inevitably ship-owners must assess the possible commercial requirements of another generation. Each of these ships has the capacity to carry cars, heavy earth-moving equipment and other cargo, including 1,040 containers, that can be maneouvred by means of a ramp at the stern. Also, the four decks can be reached by fixed ramps. For cargo handling overside, there are two

18-ton cranes, and two 25-ton and two $13\frac{1}{2}$-ton straddle carriers for coping with large steel plates and lumber. General cargo is stowed by two 20-ton fork lift trucks. To complete the specialized equipment are three vehicles: a deck-sweeping machine, a jeep and a motor cycle; the last two are for inspection of the cargo decks.

All three ships were built in Gothenburg, Sweden by Eriksberg Mekanista Werkstads AB. Their deadweight tonnage is 20,000 tons, corresponding to a cubic capacity of 1,800,000 cubic feet. They are 653 feet in length with a breadth of 94 feet; and are driven at a service speed of 22.5 knots by three Pielstick diesel engines coupled to a single screw.

The Oil/Bulk/Ore Carrier

The *Irfon* (1971) is an example of a treble-purpose cargo carrier, the first of three similar ships for the P & O Group, all to be time-chartered to Associated Bulk Carriers Limited, owned jointly by P & O and Anglo-Norness. She has a deadweight capacity of 150,100 long tons (this figure includes fuel and stores); her oil carrying capacity is 145,000 tons. With her tanks cleaned out, she has a dry cargo capacity of 5,928,000 cubic feet. This might include grain, fertilizers, bauxite and coal – all constituting cargo in bulk. Thirdly, she can become an ore carrier pure and simple, the iron ore being distributed in five of her nine holds.

The *Irfon's* overall length is 946 feet, not far short of the *Queen Elizabeth II's* length of 963 feet. Her breadth is 142 feet and draught 57 feet, when she is loaded to capacity as a dry cargo ship. Single-screw steam turbines developing 24,000 shaft horsepower drive her at a speed of $15\frac{1}{2}$ knots. The name *Irfon* is not of Continental origin, as it might seem to be, but is derived from a Welsh foxhound pack. Her builders were Howaldtswerke-Deutsche Werft in Kiel, Germany. At the time of writing, an even larger oil/ore carrier is building for the P & O Group at the Mitsubishi shipyard. The *Lauderdale* (1972) has a deadweight capacity of no less than 257,000 tons.

The Liquefied Natural Gas Carrier

The liquefied natural gas carrier is a ship type that as recently as the 1950s would have raised the eyebrows not only of the public at large but of shipowners as well. Today there is a growing demand for natural gas as a source of energy. The gas is transported in its liquid state, which is less bulky. This calls for ships of highly specialized design, able to keep the gas at the pressure and very low temperature necessary.

In 1974, Liquefied Natural Gas Carriers, a consortium formed by P & O, A.P.Møller of Denmark and Fearnley & Eger of Norway, will take delivery of their first ship of this type from the Norwegian shipyard of Moss Rosenberg AS. Possible services for this ship include Algeria, Nigeria, Venezuela and Ecuador, with linking routes to the USA. She may also trade from the Persian Gulf or Brunei to Japan. The appearance of the ship is futuristic. Five barrel-shaped structures dominate the superstructure. They are protective covers for the five tanks carrying 3,095,000 cubic feet of gas at the extraordinarily low temperature of minus 163 degrees centigrade – lower even than the shade temperature on the moon, which is about minus 112 degrees centigrade. The entire gas cargo can be discharged within twelve hours. The ship is no pup; in dimensions she comes close to the big container ships. She has a length of 816 feet, a breadth of as much as 131 feet – accounted for by the 110 feet diameter of each storage tank – and is propelled by single-screw steam turbines for a speed of 19 knots. The two boilers can burn conventional oil fuel or methane, the main constituent of natural gas.

Bibby Line in Liverpool have two ships under construction to carry liquefied petroleum gas, and when they are delivered in 1973 they will take their place in the open charter market. They are being built in the France-Gironde shipyard at Dunkerque. They will carry more than 1,600,000 cubic feet of liquefied gas at a temperature of minus 48 degrees centigrade. Their length is 676 feet, breadth 103 feet, gross tonnage 31,000 tons. Single screw 20,000 horsepower Sulzer diesel engines will give a speed of 17.5 knots.

Disasters at sea

Hard aground on rock, and within sight of shore, the troopship *Birkenhead* broke in two; the stern part sank, taking with it 648 troops and crew. The twenty women and children on board were saved.

The *Titanic*, in the charge of
tugs that were never to see
her again, sets out on her first
and last voyage.

The wooden Blackwall frigate
Cospatrick moored alongside
another sailing ship in London
docks. She is taking on board
stores and provisions for the
voyage, before moving to a
berth to load cargo – here she
is light and high out of the
water.

The Titanic (1912)

There have been disasters since man first took to the sea. Quite apart from the self-inflicted losses acquired in sea battles, those referred to here are the tragedies that overtook ships and men going about their lawful occasions.

The greatest tragedy this century was the sinking of the *Titanic* in 1912, after she struck an iceberg. Full-length books have been written; films have been made. The disaster lives on, perhaps because it happened at a period when passenger liners had grown to a size and grandeur that made them invulnerable in the public eye.

The *Titanic* was one of three sister ships that the White Star Line built in opposition to the smaller but faster *Mauretania* and *Lusitania* of the Cunard Line. They were bigger but slower ships; size and comfort were put before speed. The *Titanic* had a tonnage of 46,329 and a service speed of just over twenty-one knots, compared with the *Mauretania's* 31,938 tons and speed of twenty-five and a half knots. Her passenger capacity was 2,603, against the *Mauretania's* 2,198.

When the *Titanic* had embarked all her passengers for her maiden voyage at Southampton, Cherbourg and Queenstown, she had on board 1,316 passengers,

roughly half her complement. The date was 11 April 1912. For three days the *Titanic* headed westward towards New York on a sea that was like glass. Ice conditions in that year were exceptional; ice floes, pack ice and icebergs came unusually far south. Not every ship was equipped with wireless; many carried only one operator, who obviously could not be on continuous duty. Therefore, ice reports were sporadic.

Near midnight on Sunday, 14 April, before there was time to bring the great ship to a course to clear an iceberg dead ahead, the ship with all her bulk driving at twenty-one knots met the lethally sharp ice edge of the berg, which cut deep into her hull for a length of 300 feet.

There was no dramatic crash of collision. In his account of the loss of the ship Lawrence Beesley wrote: 'There came what seemed to me nothing more than an extra heave of the engines; no sense of shock, no jar that felt like one heavy body meeting another'.

The sea was so calm and visibility so clear that experienced seamen who gave evidence at the Courts of Enquiry said that stars close to the horizon were defined sharply enough to be taken for the mast headlights of ships. It was a night of intense cold, without wind. The *Titanic* lay still, ablaze with lights. There was no panic. The roar of the unwanted head of steam blowing off from the boilers was then the only outward sign that something was amiss. But officers and men were removing the covers from lifeboats and rockets were being fired. From the radio room the distress call 'CQD' was reaching many ships. The Cunard liner *Carpathia,* the fastest ship in the area, was fifty-eight miles away; by pushing her engines to their utmost power she reached the scene in three and a half hours. By then the *Titanic* had sunk, taking with her 1,494 passengers and crew.

The immensely long gash in her hull extended as far forward as number six boiler room; slowly the *Titanic* was settling by the bows. When the water level reached the top of the bulkhead the sea entered number five boiler room, then number four. So many

compartments of the ship were exposed to the sea that nothing could save her. The fourteen lifeboats were swung out; but they left the ship short of their full capacity. Survivors have said that hundreds of passengers simply could not believe that the *Titanic* was actually sinking. They clung on until the tilting of the ship flung them into the ice cold sea. From a lifeboat Lawrence Beesley watched the great ship tilt until her stern was upright. Her lights went out; there was a prolonged rumble as the engines and boilers broke loose from their beds, and then she slid from sight.

There were two Courts of Enquiry, in the USA and Britain. Much was made of the *Titanic's* alleged excessive speed in seas where ice and icebergs had been widely reported. Constructionally her bulkhead subdivision met the requirements of the day, as also did the lifeboats and life-saving equipment such as rafts and lifebelts. But one outcome was a series of safety recommendations concerning the subdivision of ships, the number and capacity of lifeboats, the control and administration of radio installations, and rules for speed reduction when ice and icebergs had been reported. Captain Rostron of the *Carpathia* was commended for his alacrity in reaching the area in time to save 712 people.

The Grounding of the Birkenhead (1852)

The capes that terminate the continents of South America and South Africa are the tombstones of countless numbers of men in sailing ships who died when their ship sank under them, or were swept off the yards in the act shortening sail. The Cape of Good Hope has nothing like the horrific history of Cape Horn, but the meeting of the South Atlantic and the southern part of the Indian Ocean sets up strange currents and long rolling swells.

The *Birkenhead* was one of seventeen paddle-driven iron frigates built in the 1840s that the Admiralty condemned as unserviceable as fighting ships. She was converted to a troop ship. One tragic error in the conversion process was the decision to create more spacious decks by cutting large holes and openings in the watertight bulkheads that separated them.

The *Birkenhead* had already carried troops to Canada and to Cape Town when she began another voyage to South Africa to reinforce British troops fighting a series of actions with the Kaffirs. She arrived at the naval base of Simonstown on the Cape peninsula on 23 February 1852 under the command of Captain Robert Salmond. The officer commanding troops was Major Alexander Seton. At Simonstown the *Birkenhead* filled her coal bunkers and took on

The *Morro Castle* in 1934, on fire off Asbury Park, New Jersey.

extra stores, also horses needed for military service by the army officers on board. By the evening of 25 February she was on course for Port Elizabeth, where the troops were to be disembarked. She was steaming at eight and a half knots in a flat calm in perfect visibility when she went headlong on to a reef off Danger Point. The swell and a powerful current setting towards the land had pushed her farther inshore than she should have been.

Captain Salmond ordered soundings to be taken. The ship had no more than twelve feet of water under her bows, but sixty feet at the stern, which gave her

ample buoyancy. Unbeknown to Captain Salmond however, the ship was impaled on a pinnacle of rock. He gave the order to put the engines full astern, and a huge gap was torn in the hull. The sea swept into the shattered forepart, drowning troops in the lower decks. (If the bulkheads had been left undisturbed when she was converted into a troop ship, the ship would have maintained her buoyancy.)

The situation now strained the hull so acutely that the *Birkenhead* broke in two while troops and crew were struggling to release the lifeboats on the paddle-boxes. The funnel broke loose and crushed many

men. But all the women and children were got safely away in two cutters and a gig. Major Seton had detailed sixty troops to man the pumps, others to blindfold the horses in the hope that when they were put overboard some would reach shore. Only three lifeboats remained for the 600 men still on board. The troops were ordered to maintain ranks on the poop as the ship's shattered forepart broke away. Only twenty-five minutes had passed since the *Birkenhead* had struck the reef.

Most of the troops could not swim; those that could had to struggle through seaweed, which, though in itself a potential menace, mercifully protected them from the sharks that infested the sea off Danger Point. Meanwhile the ship's mainmast remained above water and the fifty or more men with the strength to hang on were rescued by the schooner *Lionness*. Of the *Birkenhead*'s complement of 648, only 193 were saved. Captain Salmond and Major Seton were lost. The report of the senior surviving army officer, Captain Wright, ended thus: 'Everyone did as he was directed and there was not a murmur or cry among them until the vessel made her final plunge'.

The Cospatrick's Destruction by Fire (1874)

On 17 November 1874 the Blackwall frigate *Cospatrick* was under full sail in the southern Indian Ocean, well to the east of the Cape of Good Hope and bound for Auckland with 429 emigrants and a crew of forty-four. The *Cospatrick* was a well-built ship constructed of teak. She had been built in Burma in 1856 for Duncan Dunbar's fleet of ships trading between Britain and India. She sailed regularly and safely for seventeen years and then in 1873 she was sold to the Shaw, Savill Company, which was eager to buy ships for the booming emigrant trade to New Zealand. There was a good north-west wind; the *Cospatrick* was no fast clipper but she had been making a steady 200 miles a day and all was well.

In the middle watch those on deck saw smoke coming from the extreme forward end of the ship, followed instantly by tongues of flame. A fire had started in the worst possible place – the boatswain's store, stocked with paint, oil, tarred ropes and oakum. What happened next was disastrous. Possibly the forward headsails and rigging had been burnt through, for the man at the wheel lost control of the ship. The *Cospatrick* swung head to wind, which drove the fire at a furious pace down the length of the ship. There might have been a chance of saving the ship had she been kept on course with the wind behind her.

Attempts by the crew to contain the fire were

The Swedish liner *Stockholm* after her collision with the *Andrea Doria,* showing vividly the degree of impact when she penetrated the latter's hull. A US helicopter stands by.

abandoned. They were forced aft into a mass of terrified passengers. In such conditions discipline went by the board; in ninety minutes the *Cospatrick* was ablaze from stem to stern. A boat was lowered and immediately swamped and overturned by the crush of people who jumped into it. The long-boat caught fire as it was being swung out. Only two boats cleared the ship. In them were eighty-one survivors, who had the frightful experience of watching helplessly as those still alive took refuge on the poop. Already dozens had been killed when the ship's three masts, blazing furiously, crashed to the deck.

The *Cospatrick* stayed afloat for thirty-six hours. On the second day the survivors jumped over the side to their deaths, for the two lifeboats were already overloaded. The boats kept together in nights of high winds until, at dawn on 22 November, one boat was nowhere to be seen, leaving the second mate Henry MacDonald in charge of thirty-eight people, most of them in their night-clothes. They had no food, water nor even a sail – only a single oar. MacDonald rigged

sea anchors to help keep the waterlogged boat afloat. Then the oar was swept away. On 26 November, after nine days alone on the sea, the few left alive watched in despair as a ship passed them by in the last hour before dawn. Five were left. On 27 November they were rescued by the *British Sceptre*, on passage from Calcutta to Dundee. Three seamen, the second mate, and a single passenger who had been driven mad by exposure and the effects of drinking sea water, were taken on board. Two died but the second mate and two seamen recovered – only three of the 473 people who had sailed from London with such high hopes.

The Buring of the Morro Castle (1934)

Fire on board a ship at sea is a hazard that has been reduced substantially with the decreasing use of inflammable materials, such as a concentration of wood in public rooms and cabins. Fire protection and regulations for safety have included the fitting of sprinkler systems, linked to the bridge by tell-tale devices so that a fire can be identified and quickly

The last moments of the *Andrea Doria*. This picture, by Harry Trask, a photographer working for the *Boston Traveller*, won him the Pulitzer Prize for the best news photograph of the year.

extinguished. In September 1934 the American liner *Morro Castle* became a subject of special investigation (because of inconsistencies in her handling) after a fire destroyed her when she was on passage from Havana to New York with 316 passengers and a crew of 232. The *Morro Castle* was owned by the Ward Line. She was a new ship driven by turbo-electric machinery, which had a vogue in the mid-1930s. She was a fast, moderate-sized ship of 11,520 tons designed to operate a 'ferry' service between New York and Havana.

Two days out from Havana the master, Captain Wilmott, collapsed and died. During that same night of 8 September, when the ship was off the New Jersey coast, fire broke out in the library. It swept through the ship like a whirlwind. The acting master, Captain Warms, kept the ship on course at full speed, delayed sending an SOS and then inexplicably turned the ship and headed for the New Jersey shore. The change of wind drove the flames towards the fore end of the ship. Passengers were trapped in their cabins, the main staircases were ablaze, and the entire superstructure was enveloped in flames.

Coastguard cutters and salvage ships rushed to the scene, as also did the British liner *Monarch of Bermuda*, which picked up seventy-one survivors. One hundred and thirty-three died in the fire and there were many serious injuries.

Towlines were secured from the cutter *Tampa*; then a north-easterly gale set in and the *Morro Castle* was driven ashore at Asbury Park, New Jersey, in the bizarre position of being within hailing distance of Asbury Park Convention Hall. She burnt for eight days.

In February 1935 she was still aground after frequent attempts to float her. It was not until March that the hulk was refloated and towed to New York. Finally she was taken to Baltimore for breaking up. Wreck or no wreck, the *Morro Castle* was to make a last appearance in the news. She caught fire again on 28 June 1935 and fire boats and fire brigades had to be summoned to put a full stop to a sorry story.

The Collision between the Andrea Doria and the Stockholm (1956)

The collision between the Italian liner *Andrea Doria* and the Swedish liner *Stockholm* on 25 July 1956, in the sea approaches to New York, was one of those events that seem improbable at the time, because navigational aids had by then reached near-perfection.

At the height of the summer tourist season the sea tracks that lead from the Nantucket Lightship into New York, some two hundred miles distant, are crowded with passenger liners, apart from the cargo ships, tankers, and coastal craft that are there all the year round. The Nantucket is a junction of the sea, from which ships steam south towards Long Island, thence into the reaches of lower New York Bay.

For the 29,083-ton *Andrea Doria* this was the last night of her 101st Atlantic crossing. She was due in New York from Genoa early the following morning to land 1,134 passengers. Captain Piero Calamai was on the bridge. About 150 miles from the Nantucket Lightship his ship had run into fog which thickened as she drew further south.

At about that time the 12,644-ton Swedish passenger liner *Stockholm*, outward bound for Copenhagen and Gothenberg, had set course for Nantucket. The sea was calm and the visibility perfect. Weather conditions in the sea areas where the two ships were steaming could not have been more contrasting, a factor that was to bear on the approaching disaster.

The fog thickened around the *Andrea Doria*'s position; visibility was down to about half a mile, and the well-tried routine of the sea was followed in the ship. Watertight doors were closed; look-outs were posted in the bows; the whistle sounded its warning at 100-second' intervals; speed was eased from 23 knots to 21.8; and the two radar screens were under constant observation for the tell-tale 'pips' revealing the presence of another ship.

On the bridge of the *Stockholm* the watchkeeping officers and men were relieved at 8.30 pm. The ship was steaming at her customary eighteen knots; moon and stars were clearly visible. Captain Nordenson made his usual 9 pm check in the wheelhouse of course and speed. At 10.20 pm the *Andrea Doria*'s radar showed she was abreast of the Nantucket Lightship, invisible in the fog. The two ships were converging at a combined speed of more than forty knots.

From the *Stockholm* the mast headlights of the *Andrea Doria* could be seen, but not her side lights — red on the port side, green to starboard. Visibility was so reduced that on the bridge of each ship it was thought the 'rule of the road' was being followed, and that they would pass safely green to green, as the Italians believed, and red to red as the Swedes believed. To the horror of both, the ships were presenting red to green. They had both altered course towards each other. In the closing seconds before impact orders to the engine rooms were too late. The *Stockholm* with a momentum of eighteen knots tore into the hull of the *Andrea Doria*; the damage she caused was all the more severe because her bows were strengthened for navigation in ice.

Almost immediately the *Andrea Doria* took a list to starboard, a list that gradually increased, indicating a loss of stability and halving her lifeboat capacity because those on the port side could not be launched. Fortunately there were many ships in the area and the United States Coastguard Service was aptly geared to handle emergencies. Possibly the most reassuring sight to the passengers in the *Andrea Doria* was the appearance of the French liner *Ile de France*, which had left New York on the same tide as the *Stockholm*. She rescued 753 people; the *Stockholm* picked up 545, and altogether the total rescued by ships on the scene was 1,663 out of the 1,706 on board the *Andrea Doria*. To observers the *Andrea Doria*'s list was so incredibly steep that it would have been possible to walk along her port side. She remained afloat for eleven hours. Then her port side boats broke away from the hull, which disappeared in a depth of 225 feet. For three and a half months the disaster was the subject of legal argument and the case eventually was settled out of court.

The *Pamir,* one of the last of the sea-going sail-training ships.

The Loss of the Training Ship Pamir (1957)

On the continent of Europe great store was held by sail training as a method of introducing cadets to the ways of the sea, the disciplines of seamanship and ship handling. Germany was particularly keen on sail training. The best known sail-training establishment in Germany was the Deutscher Schulschiff Verein, and as recently as 1927 they commissioned a steel full-rigged ship of 1,257-tons, the *Schulschiff Deutschland*. When the sailing fleet of the Finnish shipowner Gustaf Erikson was sold after his death, Germany acquired two of his ships to train captains. One was the *Pamir*, which had been built in 1905.

The *Pamir* began her training ship career after the Second World War, carrying grain and nitrates from South America. Her normal crew was eighty-six, a high figure because fifty-two were cadets, their average age seventeen. The years passed, and by 1957 hundreds of cadets had done their stint in the *Pamir*. Early in August she put into the River Plate, loaded a full cargo of wheat, was towed clear of the land, set all sail and steered north towards the Azores. It was customary for the *Pamir* to report her position by radio at intervals, which she did on 20 September when about five hundred miles south-west of the Azores. Almost simultaneously weather stations began broadcasting warnings that a hurricane was building up west of the Cape Verde Islands.

In the *Pamir* Captain Diebitsch's barometer fell rapidly. On 22 September the ship was battling for her life in sixty-mile-an-hour winds and precipitous seas. The violent movement of the ship caused the cargo to shift, which added to the *Pamir*'s predicament for her sails were in tatters and the rigging was giving way.

The *Pamir* was in a regular sea lane and her first SOS was picked up by several ships. She continued with further messages, reporting position and condition. Then there was silence. Her last message was: 'Lost all sails. Beginning to list badly. Need help.' An American cargo ship, the *President Taylor*, was the nearest ship but when she reached the scene she found nothing, and night was falling. All day on 23 September the search was taken up by other ships and aircraft; empty lifeboats were seen. By dusk look-outs in another American ship, the *Saxon*, came upon a lifeboat with five men in it. They were the only survivors.

Bibliography

First Beginnings
The Living Past — Ivar Lissner
Jonathan Cape, London 1957 &
Putnam, New York 1961

*An Outline History of the World** — Edited by Sir John Hammerton
Amalgamated Press, London 1933

*A History of England** — Keith Feiling
Macmillan, London 1950

*The Sailing Ship** — R. & R.C. Anderson
Bonanza Books, New York 1963

*The Shipwright's Trade** — Sir Westcott Abell
Cambridge University Press 1948

*The Ship** — Björn Landström
Allen & Unwin, London 1961 &
Doubleday, New York 1967

*Sailing Ships** — Björn Landström
Allen & Unwin, London 1969 &
Doubleday, New York 1969

*Sails Through the Centuries** — S. Svensson
Macmillan, London 1962 &
Macmillan, New York 1965

The Vikings — Editors of Horizon Magazine
Cassell, London 1965

Escape from the Dark Ages
Books listed under *First Beginnings* with an asterisk, also:
The Atlantic — Leonard Outhwaite
Coward McAnn Inc., New York 1957

Three Centuries of Sail (1500–1800)
Books listed under *First Beginnings* with an asterisk, also:
The Adventure of Sail — Captain Donald MacIntyre
Elek Productions, London 1970 &
Random House, New York 1970

The Fatal Impact — Alan Moorehead
Hamish Hamilton, London 1966 &
Harper-Row, New York 1966

The Clipper Ship
The Adventure of Sail — Captain Donald MacIntyre
Elek Productions, London 1970 &
Random House, New York 1970

The Romance of the Clipper Ships — Basil Lubbock
Hennel Locke, London 1948

The China Clippers — Basil Lubbock
Brown, Son & Ferguson, Glasgow 1957

The Western Ocean Packets — Basil Lubbock
Brown, Son & Ferguson, Glasgow 1956

The Clipper Ship Era — Captain Arthur H. Clark
7 C's Press Inc., Riverside,
Connecticut, USA 1970 (Revised
edition of original published in 1910)

The Search for Speed Under Sail 1700–1855 — Howard I. Chapelle &
Norton, New York 1967 &
Allen & Unwin, London 1968

Pioneer Shipowners Vols 1 & 2 — Clement Jones, C.B.
Charles Birchall & Sons, Liverpool
1935 and 1938

The Mirror of the Sea — Joseph Conrad
Methuen, London 1906

Reminiscences of a Liverpool Shipowner — Sir William B. Forwood
Henry Young & Sons, Liverpool 1920

Clipper Ship to Motor Liner, the Story of the New Zealand Shipping Company — Sydney D. Waters
The New Zealand Shipping Company,
London 1939

The Flag of the Southern Cross, the History of Shaw, Savill & Albion Company — Frank C. Bowen
Shaw, Savill & Albion Company,
London 1939

Two Centuries of Shipbuilding 1720–1920 — Scotts at Greenock, 1920

Fighting Ships (1700–1906)
Two Centuries of Shipbuilding 1720–1920 — Scotts at Greenock, 1920

The Wooden Fighting Ship in the Royal Navy AD 897–1860 — E.H.H. Archibald
Blandford Press, London 1968 &
Arco, New York 1970

Fighting Ships — Richard Hough
Michael Joseph, London 1969 &
Putnam, New York 1969

Pictorial History of the Royal Navy, Vol. 1, 1816–1880 — Anthony J. Watts
Ian Allan, London 1970

Great Sea Battles — Oliver Warner
Weidenfeld & Nicolson, London 1963 &
International Publications Services,
New York 1963

Famous Sea Fights — J.R. Hale
Methuen, London 1911

The Defeat of the Spanish Armada — Garrett Mattingly
Jonathan Cape, London 1959 &
Houghton Mifflin, New York 1959

Nelson — Carola Oman
Hodder & Stoughton, London 1947 &
Verry, New York 1967

The Commerical Ship
From Paddle Steamer to Nuclear Ship — W.A. Baker
C.A. Watts, London 1965

The History of Merchant Shipping Vol. 4 — W.S. Lindsay
Sampson Low, London 1876

Steam Conquers the Atlantic — David B. Tyler
D. Appleton-Century Co., Inc.,
New York 1939

History of the Cunard Steamship Company — Published privately in Liverpool, 1886

Royal Mail: A Centenary History of Royal Mail Lines — T.A. Bushell
Trade & Travel Publications, London 1939

Centenary History of the P & O Line — Boyd Cable
Ivor Nicholson & Watson, London 1937

A Century of Atlantic Travel — Frank C. Bowen
Sampson Low, London 1930

Ships & South Africa — Marischal Murray
Oxford University Press, London 1933

Spanning the Atlantic, the History of the Cunard Line — F. Lawrence Babcock
Alfred A. Knopf, New York 1931

The Merchant Ship — G.S. Baker
Sigma Books, London 1948

From Slip to Sea — A.C. Hardy
Brown, Son & Ferguson, Glasgow 1935

Nuclear Ship Propulsion — Rowland F. Pocock
Ian Allan, London 1970

The Ocean Tramp — Frank C. Hendry
Collins, London 1938

Disasters at Sea
Some Sea Disasters and Their Causes — K.C. Barnaby
Hutchinson, London 1968 &
A.S. Barnes, New York 1970

The Loss of the Titanic — Philip Allan, London 1912

White Star — Roy Anderson
T. Stephenson & Son,
Prescot, Lancashire 1964

Collision Course — Alvin Moscow
Longmans, Green, London 1959 &
Putnam, New York 1959

Sea-Toll of Our Time — R.L. Hadfield
Philip Allan, London 1930

Special Purpose Ships
Chief sources were the Chamber of Shipping of the United Kingdom, and individual shipping companies, British and American

The Liner Today
The Ship — Björn Landström
Allen & Unwin, London 1961 &
Doubleday, New York 1967
Other sources included the Chamber of Shipping of the United Kingdom; J.D. Prince, Editor, *Lloyd's List*; The Shipping World; The Motor Ship; and Fairplay Publications

Freaks
The Great Iron Ship — James Dugan
Harper, New York 1953

Freak Ships — Stanley Rogers
Bodley Head, London 1936

Bizarre Ships of the Nineteenth Century — John Guthrie
Hutchinson, London 1970

Index

Acknowledgements

The authors and publishers are most grateful to the following individuals and organizations for their help in supplying illustrations for use in this book.

Giovanni Agosto, page 103
American Museum, Bath and Michael Holford, page 78
Author's collection, pages 103, 108, 110–111, 112, 113 (2), 114, 141
Stewart Bale, pages 94, 100, 101, 104
Raymond Balfour, pages 16 (2), 17 (2)
Barnaby's Picture Library, pages 41, 73, 91, 105
Ben Line, pages 130–131
Brian Brake, pages 4–5
Camera Press, pages 9, 75, 77
Edward Clapham, page 28
Danish Embassy, page 102
Mike Davis, pages 49, 52–53, 56, 92–93
Deutsche Atlantic Linie, page 107
Elsam, Mann and Cooper, page 101
Eriksberg Mek. Verkstads AB, Gothenburg, page 106
An Esso Photograph, page 128
Mary Evans Picture Library, pages 15, 28, 67 (2), 68, 84, 95, 122
Fox Photos, page 59
John R. Freeman, page 51
Furness Withy Group, page 135
Greene Line Steamers Inc., page 126
Hines Inc., page 129
Michael Holford, page 56
Holland America Line, page 108
Hong Kong Government Information Services, back flap of jacket
Hull Museums, page 21
Imperial War Museum, page 84
Keystone Press, pages 88, 89
Lloyd's Lists, page 105
Magdalene College, Cambridge, page 48
Mansell Collection, pages 10, 12–13, 15, 26–27, 29, 30 (2), 31, 43, 46, 47 (2), 56, 72, 81, 84, 90 (2), 91, 94, 117, 118, 119, 120–121, 133
Mariners Museum, Newport News, pages 61, 80, 96
Montagu Motor Museum, pages 57, 82–83
National Maritime Museum, Greenwich, pages 26 (3), 27 (3), 29, 44–45, 57, 64
National Maritime Museum, Greenwich and Michael Holford, pages 12, 49, 53, 61, 87, 96
National Portrait Gallery, page 55 (2)
New Zealand High Commission, page 34
Octopus Books, pages 18, 32–33, 34, 36, 37, 41, 62, 92 (3), 98, 116, 127 (4)
Parker Gallery, pages 2–3, 60, 79, 83, 86
P & O Line, pages 74–75, 112, 114
P & O Anglo-Norness, page 106
Picturepoint, pages 18, 19, 35
Popperfoto, pages 20–21, 22, 30, 54, 68–69, 85, 103, 115, 134, 136–137, 138, 139
Portuguese Tourist Office, pages 39, 40, 42
Royal Scottish Museum, Edinburgh, page 46
Schleswig-Holsteinischer Landsmuseums, Schleswig, page 25
Science Museum, London, pages 11, 38, 51, 54, 58, 76, 90, 91, 95
G. T. Severin, page 126
Shell Photo Service, page 123
Sing Tao Newspapers, Hong Kong, back endpapers
Skyfotos Ltd., page 109
Smithsonian Institution, page 63
Southern Newspapers, page 104
Streckfus Steamers Inc., pages 124–125
Universitetets Oldsaksamling, Oslo, half title, pages 23, 25
Wasavarvart, page 50
Wide World Photos, page 104